TENEMENT DWELLERS

*Anecdotes and Tales
From the Old Neighborhood*

TENEMENT DWELLERS

*Anecdotes and Tales
From the Old Neighborhood*

Lawrence - My Hometown
Richard Edward Noble

Copyright © 2011 by Richard Edward Noble

All rights reserved. No part of this book may be reproduced in any form or by any electronic or mechanical means, including information storage or retrieval systems without permission from the publisher.

Published in the United States of America
By
Noble Publishing
889 C.C. Land Road
Eastpoint, Florida 32328
richardedwardnoble@fairpoint.net

Interior layout and design by
Carol Noble

Dedication

This book is dedicated to Louise Sandberg and the Friends of the Lawrence Public Library. Louise and the many Friends of the Lawrence Public Library found me somehow in their search for local writers. To garner the interest of *library people* should be an inspiration to any struggling writer. It certainly was to me. When they chose one of my titles, *Just Hangin' Out, Ma* to sell as a part of their fund raising efforts, I was thrilled. Thank-you all so very much. You are all appreciated.

Introduction

Tenement Dwellers is the second volume of anecdotes in my projected series of books about the old neighborhood and growing up in a collapsing, forgotten, industrial mill town along the Eastern seaboard of the United States.

Lawrence, Massachusetts was my hometown. It was seven square miles of three-decker tenement houses, housing projects, kids and congestion. It was schoolyards, churches, smokestacks, pool halls, back alleys, barrooms and mile after mile of abandoned, redbrick mill buildings.

My best times growing up in the 40's, 50's and 60's in Lawrence were those many hours spent with my childhood buddies hangin' out on the street corners, shooting hoops in the schoolyards and just idling here and there.

Lawrence was a forgotten town and we were its offspring. We were not only forgotten, we were ignored and avoided. But in that abandonment we kids found companionship and camaraderie. We discovered the intricacies of friendship, breaking chops and having fun.

I have no definition of the term love other than friendship. I learned it as a tenement dweller hanging on the periphery of a social disaster with my buddies. I learned it hiding from the cold in a stranger's hallway, sitting on the wall up at the Howard playstead, shooting hoops under a streetlight or going out of my way to walk a buddy halfway home in a snow storm on a late evening.

I've had a good life, making friends wherever I've gone and I'm still at it. Enjoy this book, my friends. If you don't learn anything from it, I do hope you at least get a few laughs.

Contents

Chip off the Old Beer Bottle ... 11
Ed's Quality Market ... 15
My Name's Tucker ... 22
Brother Kenneth Robert ... 29
Me and Charles Dickens ... 34
Dirty Dancing ... 39
Radio Days ... 44
Jimmy and His Dog Tige ... 49
Martha, the Preacher's Daughter ... 55
Kirby Vacuum Cleaner Salesman ... 61
Lennie's on the Turnpike ... 68
Barbershops ... 73
Barrooms ... 78
Evolution of Heat ... 82
Gambling ... 86
Hopping Cars ... 92
Sewer Covers ... 95
Hangin' Out as Therapy ... 99
The Frolics ... 105
Mister Five by Five ... 109
Basketball Be My life ... 114
Strip Joints ... 120
Alma Meter ... 124
English with Brother Stanislaus ... 130
The Infamous Pothole ... 134
Canobie Lake Park ... 139

Hart's Package Store ... 143

Shooting Pool and Bowling for Dollars ... 147

Lawton's By the Sea ... 152

Costy's Back Yard ... 157

Somebody's Got to Lose ... 162

The Merry Mac Club ... 167

Big Town – Small Town ... 171

Good Old Dr. Lemmings ... 175

Chip off the Old Beer Bottle

 Lawrence and frugality are synonyms to me. Penuriousness and parsimony are so common that they should be considered as street names in my hometown of Lawrence, Massachusetts. Cheap and penny pinching are complimentary adjectives in every Lawrencian's handbook. They can call it what they want but it is all thriftiness and good old New England shopping in our book of proverbs.
 Waste not, want not, charity begins at home and a penny saved, is a penny earned are simply statements of revealed, profound truth. I'm sure they must be in the Bible – if not the Bible, in Ben Franklin's Almanac which is a close second to the Bible.
 The only person in the world who can upset me with adjectives like cheap or tightwad is my wife. But whenever she does, she knows what she is in for.
 The litany begins with the Maine lobster stuffed with real Alaskan king crab meat that I bought for her on our first real date at the big, fancy Fishermen's restaurant in Fort Lauderdale. I even took the car to the valet parking that evening back in 1972. That is the year 1972 when a dollar was a dollar and a fifty cent tip to the valet parking guy meant something. It meant something to me anyway.
 Then we jump right up to my demand that we go all the way and buy a brand, new mobile home for $8,886 back in

1982 rather than buy a used mobile home for less than half that price.

The matching towel rack and toilet paper holder, made out of real wood, imported all the way from China as opposed to the plastic one that was on sale at Kmart at the time is another glaring instance of my wild and crazy extravagant nature when it came to caring for my loved one(s).

Need I even mention my insistence on all-beef, no-name brand hot dogs or my demand that we buy raisins at the Dollar General Discount Store to add to our no-name bran flakes? Come on now? Let's not just throw around those derogatory adjectives without a little forethought here. I could go on and on but I think I have made my point.

But getting away from my tendency towards conspicuous consumption and my periods of extravagance in the name of love and responsibility and returning to the topic at hand – reasonable and thought-out conservative spending, I ask myself, "Where did I get such an educated economic nature?"

I got it from my friends on the street corner, their parents, the local shop owners, the little red school house I attended, the good nuns and from vivid examples that took place right in my tiny kitchen on 32 Chelmsford St. in uptown/downtown Lawrence, Massachusetts. For example:

My dad returns to his bit of paradise at 32 Chelmsford St. with his six pack of Holihan's Black Horse Ale under his arm. It has been a long day working as an attendant and assistant manager at the Merit gas station up on Broadway.

He was looking forward to a cold one, a pipeful of cherry scented Edgeworth tobacco and a quiet evening in front of the Zenith TV watching Ed Sullivan's *Toast of the Town* featuring strongman, Joe Banomo, who was going to dead lift the entire Ed Sullivan Show – guests and staff,

Ed and Edgar Bergen included. All in all, it was destined to be a pretty darn exciting evening.

He puts his Texaco style gas station attendant's hat on top of the refrigerator. (We are the men from Texaco ... we work from Maine to Mexico...) He deposits his beer in the refrigerator pulling the cold ones to the front and sliding the warmer ones to the rear. After bath (we had no shower in those days) and change of clothes, he returns to the refrigerator in a fresh pair of boxer shorts and a spiffy clean tank top T-shirt.

(Did I ever tell you the story about when my twelve year old sister was just learning to darn socks and hand sew, and she discovered that all of my dad's boxer shorts were torn in the front?)

Well anyway, he pulls that first nice, cold Holihan's Black Horse Ale off the shelf and saunters over to the sink. He grabs up his trusty bottle opener and pops off that first cap.

"Oh damn," he exclaims. "Will you look at this, Mary? I chipped the darn bottle top. What do I do now?"

"Well, Ernie, if I were you I would just dump that beer down the sink and get a fresh one. You don't want to take the chance on swallowing a piece of glass."

My dad leaned on the sink bracing himself with both hands and both arms, his head bowed in disgust. How could he have done such a thing? How many bottles of beer had he opened in his lifetime without a mishap – 47 million? Wow, this was a true tragedy. The silence was awesome. The struggling look, caused by the necessity to think that this accident had precipitated, was visibly painful. He pondered. He made gruesome faces. He rubbed his chin and turned around in little circles. He came to rest with his backside to the counter where his beer with the chip of glass was sitting. He then lifted his head and stared up at the buzzing florescent kitchen light with the dangling pull string for a sign.

And then it happened. The pain vanished and a look of genuine genius swept down his face – from wrinkled brow to puckered chin. He ran to his bedroom and returned with a clean linen handkerchief. My mother was watching skeptically with her arms across her chest.

My dad got his favorite, large pilsner glass off the shelf and placed it on the sink counter. He snapped open his handkerchief like he was about to perform a magic act. He draped the handkerchief over the pilsner glass as if he were in the process of making it disappear. He grasped the glass along with the handkerchief – holding the handkerchief snug around the glass. He picked up his bottle of beer and then poured the beer into the glass, straining the beer through the handkerchief that was over the top of the glass acting like a filter. The glass filled up with beer and low and behold there was the shard of glass sitting on the taut handkerchief stretched over the rim of the glass.

Holy cow! What a stroke of genius.

My dad beamed. My mom frowned and shook her head negatively.

"What?" my dad bellowed.

"What?" my mother mocked. "You just wasted a 75 cent linen handkerchief to save a darn 25 cent bottle of beer. Great goin' Albert Einstein."

My dad's beam of genius went from high to low to off. He shrugged, tossed the 75 cent handkerchief into the trash and headed to the parlor.

When my dad disappeared into the parlor with his miracle beer my mom went over and snatched the handkerchief from the trash and laughed. She looked down at me "Your father, the genius, doesn't know about the invention of the washing machine either."

Ed's Quality Market

I was working part time at Ed's Quality Market on Broadway. It was a mid-sized supermarket. Bigger than a corner store but smaller than a First National or a Stop & Shop.

Eddie Solomon was the owner and he was running the place alone. Eddie, like many of the ethnic shops in Lawrence had his nucleus of loyal customers and then branched out into the general populous.

Eddie's thriving little corner supermarket had devolved as the neighborhood deteriorated over the years and by this time most of Eddie's branches had broken off. He was now down to his treasured nucleus once again.

The bulk of his business was via the telephone and he delivered. He had a high school kid who delivered the boxes of groceries to people's doorsteps – first, second and third floor doorsteps. I know my friend Peter Shaheen worked as a delivery boy for Eddie while in high school. My experiences at Eddie's Market came some years later.

The orders started rolling in on Wednesdays and Thursdays and by Saturday Eddie had a few loads all boxed up and ready for the old station wagon/panel truck. Eddie was hanging in there, scratching by, but the handwriting was on the wall.

Eddie was running the place alone because his associate butcher of many, many years had died or retired. Eddie made a deal with me to help him out on weekends.

I had developed my own home delivery business. It all started because Steve Brennan the owner of the meat packing house where I worked gave us workers a break on our groceries. We got whatever we wanted wholesale instead of retail. I noticed that most of the married guys at the shop were buying two or three times the meat and cold cut groceries as I was. I started taking orders from some of my buddies. Then I started selling it in wholesale quantities to friends and acquaintances. Very soon I had my own little wholesale business. I was buying and cutting up large chunks or sections of meat for friends and relatives during my lunch hour, after work and on Saturdays. Eventually I had too much business and I had to hunt a new alternative. That's when I got introduced to Eddie Solomon.

Poor Eddie was now chained to the family market. He offered me the use of his market and facilities to order, store and package meat for my customers in return for helping him out and watching his business with him a couple of days a week. Now he could run out for an hour or two once in a while or take care of family business while I watched the shop. He insisted on paying me something which is one indication of the kind of person he was – and still is, I'm sure. I didn't need it. I was doing well enough on my own. I had one fulltime job, a part time job and my home meat business on the side. Eddie's would be my second part time job. Not to mention, I was single and still living at home. The arrangement was working out great for me. Eddie was happy too.

This short period that I worked at Ed's Quality Market for Eddie Solomon surprisingly holds a lot of good memories for me. I learned to admire Eddie. Number 1, he was a great boss. Well, he wasn't a boss at all. He was a friend.

He didn't need me for anything. He just wanted a little company and a tiny bit of freedom. All his store work he could do himself. He watched what I was up to and I watched him.

I had the best of this deal. I had free access to Eddie's walk-in cooler, his bandsaw, his cutting blocks, his hamburger grinder, his cold cut slicer, his cubing machine even his knives. I told him he didn't have to pay me anything for helping him out. The use of his facilities was more than payment enough on his part – but he insisted. I think he paid me 30 bucks for Friday evening and all day Saturday.

I was making pretty good money for a young guy back in those days. I remember one day a customer of Eddie's came in and wanted to cash his Social Security check. Eddie asked how much it was. It was close to 300 bucks.

"Can't help you, pal," Eddie said. "I haven't taken in 300 dollars today my friend."

"Wait a minute," I said. "I'll cash that for you." I carried hundreds of dollars in my wallet, sometimes even a thousand or two. I paid cash for everything. Paying cash got me discounts at the wholesale house. Everybody liked cash back in those days. A thousand dollars cash was a thousand dollars cash – no taxes, no bookkeeping and no check bouncing. I bought when I got a bargain and then I called my customers and sold what I had just bought. It was a good deal for me and a great deal for my customers. Not that good for the Internal Revenue Service or my future Social Security old age pension check.

Eddie was rather surprised but he didn't say anything. From then on when any of his customers came in with checks larger than he could cash, he would look at me and ask, "Dick, can you do $400?"

"Sure."

I didn't think much about it but Eddie would shake his head in disbelief.

When I decided to open up my own shop Eddie asked me, "Tell me Dick, how much are you making here a week doing this business of yours?" I didn't really want to say because I didn't know where this was going.

"I'm doing all right," I said.

"You making more than a 100 a week?" he asked. I laughed.

"You making more than 200 a week?" I smiled. Eddie shook his head. "You making more than 300 a week?"

"Sometimes."

"Dick, let me tell you something. I ain't making that much a week running this whole place. You don't want to open your own business. You want to come with me. I'm going to close this place down and open up a delicatessen on Lawrence St. I'm going to sell cooked food ready to take home and eat – spinach pies, kebbe, gourmet take out. I teach cooking classes over at the high school in the evenings. Everybody loves my stuff. It's the future. Nobody has the time to cook anymore, everybody's working, mom and dad both. The money is in prepared foods. I'll teach you how to cook. You can run your little business on the side. You'll have all the money you want."

In retrospect, I always regretted not taking that offer. I really liked working with Eddie. As it turned out I did become a chef, but I think I would have enjoyed preparing Eddie's cuisine rather than the French crème sauces that I learned. I still get hungry for stuffed grape leaves or a kebbe sandwich but I never get hungry for a bowl of shrimp and scallop bisque, or hollandaise sauce on my sautéed Sea Bass or Black Grouper. I have yet to prepare myself a Salmon fillet with a caper sauce or Blackened Redfish topped with sweet cream basil butter at home. I don't care about beurre blank, béarnaise, béchamel, bordelaise, meuniere, mirepoix, or even monosodium glutamate but I still get hungry for a Syrian salad with that unique and distinctive lemon dressing Eddie's mom used to make for us.

His mother would cook at the market for us. I think she cooked for Eddie every day – maybe every day of his life. I was invited to eat whenever I was there. She wouldn't tell me what she was making our supper from until after I ate it. Everything was wonderful. I ate tripe and lamb brains and stuffed intestines and hearts and every kind of crazy thing. Eddie even got me to start eating hamburger and steak ... raw – a practice not recommended in today's world. I never tried the lamb's eyeballs – that was a bridge a little too far. My parents being a combination of Irish and Polish, I got a thousand and one ways to cook cabbage at home. Eating at Eddie's with his mom as our cook was like dining out for lunch at some exotic restaurant. She was a little Bishop's restaurant all by herself.

I also liked the way Eddie dealt with family. Here he was a businessman but it was family before business. My dad was just a laborer but it was always job before family. I had never seen a family like Eddie's. There was more touching, hugging, kissing and laughing than I had ever seen in my life. They even seemed to enjoy their relatives.

As a businessman Eddie knew all the jokes and all the little tricks. One idea I never forgot was the Sweetheart roast beef. Eddie had a Sweetheart roast beef, a Honeymoon special, a Mother-in-law's delight and a host of other unique specials.

The first time I heard him explaining his Sweetheart Special to a young woman, I couldn't believe it. After the young woman bought her Sweetheart Special roast beef, I asked Eddie, "What the hell is a Sweetheart roast beef? I've been working as a butcher now for several years; I got all the information from the USDA; I know the name and section of every slice of steak and cut of beef on a steer but I have never heard of a Sweetheart Special."

"No you haven't. But if you buy one you will love it and you will want to get another one. When you go to the big supermarket or to that other butcher shop and ask for it, they won't have it. So then what?"

"I go back to Eddie's."

"That's right. And you will not be comparing the price of Eddie's Sweetheart roast and buying a cheaper one anywhere else because they won't know what you are talking about."

The young lady who bought the Sweetheart roast was back a few weeks later. She said, "You know, I can not buy this Sweetheart roast anywhere. I live across town and I've gone to all the butcher shops in my area and none of them have a Sweetheart roast beef." Eddie looked over at me and winked.

"Really, I'm surprised. It's a favorite with all my customers."

"Do they have another name for it that other butchers would recognize?"

"Well, in some sections of the country it is called a Honeymoon roast but I really don't know why any butcher worth his salt wouldn't know what a Sweetheart roast is. What do you think about that Dick?"

"I can't imagine. These guys must be from another planet. Sweetheart roast ... that's the favorite of 7 out of every 10 butchers I know."

She left with a Sweetheart roast and a pair of His and Her Sirloins and a Works-in-any-pot pot-roast.

"Those His and Her Sirloins are cut from a muscle never used by the steer, hidden under the spline and the Works-in-any-pot pot-roast comes from the hintermost section of the animal. If you can't get over here next time, just ask the guy at the big supermarket about the spline or the hintermost and he should fix you right up."

"Oh great. Thank-you so much. The spline and the hintermost, I'll remember that."

The next time she came in she ordered her Eddie favorites, humbly, and with no silly questions.

My Name's Tucker and I'm a Mean Mother F…..

I was casually strolling down Center St. heading towards Nell's Variety, when these three little squirts came running out from the yard next to Jack Sheehy's house. One of the little buggers tossed a rock at me. "Hey watch it you little punk or I'll come over there and teach the whole bunch of you squirts a lesson."

The little kids were about 6 or 7 years of age and I was about 10 or 12.

"Oh yeah? My big brother and his gang will kill you, man."

"Oh really? Well I have a gang too and anytime your big brother and his dumb gang wants a fight, tell them to come on down to Nell's Variety. And tell them to pack a lunch because it will be an all day affair."

"Oh yeah! My brother is Danny Tucker and he is a mean mother f----r."

"Well tell your brother Danny Tucker the mean mother f----r that Rich Noble thinks that Danny Tucker is an all day sucker."

The kids went running off and I continued on down the road to Nell's. When I got there several of the guys were sitting on the steps of the tenement adjacent to the store. "Any of you guys know some punk by the name of Tucker, Danny Tucker?"

"Danny Tucker? Yeah I know him. He hangs around up at Perrault's Diner," said Jack Sheehy.

"No kidding?"

Perrault's Diner was a bad place. A lot of bad guys hung out there. It was second only to Frank's Diner on Lawrence St. for having the meanest bunch of pre-adult potential murders, killers, thieves, drug addicts and homicidal maniacs in town. The real bad guys hung out at these diners. These type diners were where bad younger guys auditioned for their future membership at adult bad places like the Brass Rail and Pinky's. Of course, compared to us guys at Nell's everybody was mean and dangerous.

"I think I just made a big mistake. Some little kid threw a rock at me and I yelled at him and he said he was going to get his big brother after me. He said his brother was Danny Tucker the mean mother f----r."

"Oh God, you did make a big mistake. I think Danny Tucker just got out of the Pen for raping his mother and sister after he killed and ate a neighbor's pet bulldog. He is about 30 years old for criss sake. He's dangerous. I think he is a druggie too. You are in big trouble Nobes," explained my buddy Willie, laughing all the while.

"Well, I'm afraid there are more than just me in trouble. I also told the little shit that if his big brother, Danny Tucker the mean mother f----r and his gang were looking for a fight they ought to come down to Nell's. I said my gang could whip his brother's gang and that his brother and his buddies better pack a lunch because it would be an all day affair."

"WHAT! You are KIDDING? You didn't say that. Tell me you didn't say that?" petitioned my buddy Willie … now a bit more concerned.

"No that's pretty much what I said. I also said that I thought that Danny Tucker the mean mother f----r was really Danny Tucker the all day sucker."

"I think we had better get the hell out of here," offered Ray Dolan.

"What are we going to do?" Willie yelled.

"Hide man. We better find a place to hide and quick."

"I wouldn't really worry about it," said Jack Sheehy reaching rather nervously into his shirt pocket for a pack of cigarettes.

"Why not?" asked Willie.

"Because those guys are way too big for us. I mean those guys are all like a hundred years old man. They all drive cars. Some of them are married and have kids who have already been in and out of prison."

"Really?"

"Really. If they came down here and beat up us little guys they would be the laughing stock of the whole city. I mean what kind of big tough guys beat up a bunch of little kids? They ain't goin' to bother us," Jack assured as he lit his cigarette.

"Why the hell is your hand shaking like that then?" I asked.

"My hand ain't shakin'," Jack said. "Look, I'm as steady as a rock." He held his hand out in front of him and it was wiggling like a leaf in the wind. This was worse than any of us could imagine. Jack was the toughest one of our bunch. If Jack was scared, we were dead meat.

Well, there we were, we had Joe Lewis after us – we couldn't run and we couldn't hide. What should we do? We sat on the steps at Nell's thinking seriously and wringing our hands until it started to get dark and the streetlight came on.

All of a sudden a hotrod pulled up and screeched to a halt right in front of Alma Meter's house across the street from Nell's. There were two older teenagers in the front seat. "You guys better run. The gang from Perrault's is all riled up and they are on their way down here to kick the crap out of you guys." The car then peeled out from in front of Alma Meter's and then skidded around the corner at Hampshire St. We were barely off our butts when cars filled with the Perrault's gangsters began skidding around every corner. They were coming to get us from every direction. We didn't have a chance but we all ran anyway. We had no exit strategy – a few of us headed up Exchange St, a couple headed towards the Arlington Club and me and Willie ran down Exchange St. towards St. Rita's school.

Halfway down Exchange St., there was a field on the right. At the back of the field there was a tall chainlink fence with barbed wire on the top. We had cut through that field and climbed that barbed wire fence a million times. We knew just how to do it. I was in the lead and Willie was about five or ten yards behind me. I leaped up the chainlink fence, placed one foot onto the barbed wire and then leaped clear to the ground. I scrambled to my feet and I was off and running.

I didn't get ten yards before I heard my buddy Willie screaming. "Nobes, Nobes! Help me; I'm stuck."

I turned around and there was my little chum hanging upside-down. He leaped but didn't clear the barbed wire. He got one of the rolled up cuffs on his Levi's hooked onto a barb. Twenty million times we leaped this fence with no problem, now when it counts, my pal screws up.

To be quite honest, I was mighty scared. These guys from Perrault's were big and mean. They would like nothing better than to bust a few arms and legs – maybe worse than that.

Willie is trying like hell to get his cuff loose but he can't. He is trying to twist himself like a pretzel and climb back up the fence, but no luck.

I make a move to run back to the fence and get my buddy unhooked. I take no more than two steps and a Perrault's Diner car screeches and skids to a halt out on the road at Exchange St.

"There's two of the little bastards. Let's get 'em."

All the doors on the car fly open and about six of the Perrault gang start running towards us – knuckles and chains dragging.

Willie is still upside-down but he can see them coming. He twists his head and looks at me cockeyed. I can still see the desperate look in his upside-down eyeballs to this day. He was scared out of his wits. I looked at the Perrault's guys coming through the field. I looked at Willie hanging there helplessly. Instantly, without the slightest hesitation, I decided to do the right thing – the only thing.

I turned and started running away from Willie for my life. But just as I got boogieing on down that road toward abandonment of *the Willie*, I heard him cry out. His wail reminded me of a cow being bludgeoned to death on the cement slab of a slaughter house floor. It was horrifying. I looked at him hanging there upside-down and I just started laughing.

"Stop laughing you butthead and get me off this fence," he screamed, humorlessly.

I scurried back to the fence, grabbed Willie around the middle and heaved him up and down until I ripped his pant leg loose. The bad guys were right there. They were RIGHT THERE! Two of them made a running leap up the other side of the fence. Me and Willie were off and running for our lives.

I'm running and I'm scared to death but I can't stop laughing. Willie is running next to me and he starts laughing because he is listening to me laugh. But we are both still running like crazy. I take a quick gander over my shoulder and there's two of the Perrault guys hanging upside-down with their pant legs tangled in the barbed wire and the rest of them are still on the wrong side of the fence peeling their bananas and hooting, grunting and scratching under their armpits.

Willie and I stopped to catch our breath and then we got brave.

"You big, dumb screw-ups. Don't you even know how to get over a barbed wire fence? All you clowns should be back in jail where you belong; you're too stupid to be free."

"Yeah right! You're a bunch of clowns and you're all stupid. If brains were an elevator, you dopes couldn't get out of the basement and ..."

"We better get truckin' before one of them boneheads gets loose."

We were off and running for our lives once again. We cut through several yards and over a few garbage can sheds and eventually worked our way to safety. We stopped under a streetlight up on Arlington St.

"What the hell were you laughing at?" Willie panted while bent over and leaning on his thighs.

"I saw you hanging there upside-down and you looked so funny."

"Yeah really!"

"But the funniest part was, here come the bad guys and I looked at you and I said to myself, screw him. When the Perrault guys get him they will all start beating him up and I can get enough time to get away."

"Nobes, that is not funny. That is not something to laugh about. You could have got me killed."

"Yeah, but I would have got away."

"Well, my God, you're a good buddy."

"What do you mean, I came back and got you didn't I?"

"Yeah but you had to think about it."

"I know. That's what was so funny. I had to think about it. I felt like Jack Benny, you know, the thief says, 'Your money or your life.' Benny stutters and stalls. 'Well?' the bad guy demands. 'I'm thinking about it. I'm thinking about it,' says Benny."

"Well, I hope you have thought about it enough this time so that if there is a next time you will know exactly what to do."

"I have. I definitely know what to do next time. Next time you are going to be left hanging on the damn fence and I am going to get away clean. Did you see how close those guys were? Man, I almost got myself killed tryin' to save your dumb butt. I must have been delirious or something."

"You're delirious all right, pal. Take it from me, delirious has nothing on you."

Brother Kenneth Robert

In this life we are constantly making judgments about one another. Does he or doesn't he? Will she or won't she?

We are forever choosing whether to make a friend of someone or let them pass by.

Being raised in Lawrence brought these day to day decisions to a higher level. Growing up in Lawrence, I asked questions like: Is this person safe to know? If we were out drinking together and I go to the bathroom, will this person steal any money that I have left on the bar? Is this person tough or is he actually violent and physically dangerous? Insanity being a given in Lawrence, is this person simply ha-ha, hee-hee crazy or is he criminally insane? Would he eat a live pigeon while sitting on a park bench at the Common? If I disagree with this person will he become violent and try to kill me or throw me out a second or third floor window? Does this person have a trigger mechanism? For example if I say the word *mother* or *sex* or *golumpki* does saliva begin to dribble from a lower lip or does mucus start seeping from this person's nose. If I date this Lawrence girl and then decide I'm not interested, will she bring her father's police revolver to Mass on Sunday and clean it in a pew where I must watch?

Lawrence was different. After I left Lawrence it took a year or two for me to realize that most other males will not kill you just because your back is turned. When out to eat or on the town, it isn't absolutely necessary to sit with your back to a wall ... which brings me to the story of Brother Kenneth Robert.

Brother Kenneth Robert was sick. This Marist Brother was the overseer of my freshman or sophomore year homeroom. He appeared basically normal but he had a thing about food.

Being my homeroom teacher, he also supervised our study period. Study period came before lunch period. Many children in my homeroom class were hungry by the time study period rolled around and could not wait for lunch period to begin eating their lunch. If Brother Kenneth witnessed anyone nibbling a baloney sandwich, or gobbling a slab of chocolate cake during study period, he went bonkers.

Who would have known? Most other brothers could care less but Brother Kenneth was another story.

I did my homework during study period. I was busy scribbling out my geometry when I witnessed Brother Kenneth having his first episode.

I looked up and there he was steaming down the row of desks next to mine. He stopped at the kid sitting beside me. "Are you eating?" he demanded.

"No Brother. I'm not," blubbered Nicolas Lippoli. Nicolas' mouth was full and even saying these few words spattered particles of chocolate cake all over the front of Brother Kenneth's tunic. Brother Kenneth immediately shifted into "nutty" and began beating poor Nicolas. This first seizure culminated with Brother Kenneth demanding that Nicolas spit the remainder of his cake out of his mouth. Nicolas puked up his cake into the napkin his mother had wrapped it in. He then followed Brother Kenneth's mandate and deposited his semi-digested cake into a nearby trash can.

Well, that was a little strange, but not completely insane. As the year progressed Brother Kenneth evolved from a basic neurotic with violent tendencies to a definite psychotic with psychopathic seizures and blackouts. When he attacked John Pellegrino for eating his tuna on pumpernickel during study period, I thought he was going to kill the poor kid. He slapped him; he punched him; he kneed him. He knocked his desk over and then punched and kicked him while the kid was trying to squirm away along the classroom floor.

Now other than watching mom and dad at home, I had never seen people act this way in a public setting. This brother was auditioning for *One Flew Over the Cuckoo's Nest*.

When John Pellegrino came to school that next day, he had a shiner and several Band-Aids here and there. I remember thinking at that time about the spare-the-rod-and-spoil-the-child notion. Certainly one should not be eating a tuna on pumpernickel with a kosher dill pickle on the side during study period but should a grown adult be punching, kicking and scratching a medium sized boy for such an offence?

Finding such questions beyond my ethical evaluations at that stage, I decided to move on.

Christmas break was on the way and to my shock and disbelief there was John Pellegrino at my desk with an envelope. "Hey, we're all chipping in a quarter to buy Brother Kenneth a Christmas present. Do you want to chip in?"

I must admit, I found John's attitude surprising. "You're collecting quarters to buy Brother Kenneth a Christmas present?" I asked dubiously.

"Well," he smirked. "It's going to be a joke. We're getting him a wallet."

"A wallet?"

"Yeah. Brothers take a vow of poverty, you know. They can't have any money. We're getting him a wallet to break his chops."

"In that case count me in. Here you go." I gave him my quarter.

The day before our Christmas vacation, Pellegrino slipped up to Brother Kenneth's desk before study period began. He dropped a long thin package onto the desk. The package was all decked out in Christmas paper with Santa stickers and a bright red ribbon and bow. The whole class sat clandestinely, smirking but trying to act normal.

Brother Kenneth came into the room sporting his usual grumpy, warden's face. He stepped up onto the platform where his desk was located. Immediately he spotted the gift. There was an envelope with a card attached. He reached hesitantly for the card. He removed the card from the envelope and read it. He stood frozen, captured by the sentiment. When he looked up at the class tears were streaming down his cheeks. He started bawling like a baby. He turned his back to the class and fumbled inside his tunic searching for a hanky. He blew his nose and wiped his eyes. He took a few minutes to compose himself then walked around to the front of his desk. He sat on the edge of the desk. The room was quiet. We were all shocked. Everyone was rolling their eyes and shrugging their shoulders in disbelief.

"You know," said Brother Kenneth turning the package over in his hands. "All this time I thought that you guys didn't even like me." Everybody laughed and looked cross-eyed at one another. "No really, some of the other brothers told me that they had received gifts from their students but I never thought in my wildest dreams that you guys would buy me something." He choked up and started crying again. "I don't know what to say," he bawled.

After an awkward silence, Pellegrino yelled, "Open up your present, Brother." And then Pellegrino snickered. The rest of us sat there dismayed and guilty. Brother Kenneth would open it up; see that it was a wallet and then realize that the whole thing was a joke. What would he do then?

He fumbled like a two year old ripping off the bow and the ribbon and then the Santa Christmas paper. When he saw that it was a wallet, he beamed. "Oh my gosh, what a beautiful wallet! I know that you guys probably don't realize this but as a Marist Brother we all take a vow of poverty, so I don't have any money to put into this wallet. But I have family pictures of my brothers and sisters and my mom and dad that I can put in here. You guys have made the best Christmas I have ever had. This is the first year that I won't be seeing my family at Christmas time and you're my first homeroom class ever. My dad passed away last year and my brothers and sisters are all grown and off on their own. But now – thanks to you guys – I can have everybody right here in my very own wallet. I'll never forget you guys and this kindness." He put his head down and rushed out of the classroom overcome and weeping.

We were all stunned. We sat there staring up at the desk where Brother Kenneth had been standing. Then, just as if someone had given a cue or pulled a string, we all turned and stared at Pellegrino. He stared back roaming from one stern face to the next. He then threw his arms up in the air. "How the hell would I know?" he grumbled apologetically. "I didn't even think the big pr-k had a mother and father."

Me and Charles Dickens
Selling Hats

Every time I think of this story I laugh. It seems so Dickensian. What I like best about this story is there is no rush for me to write it. No one is going to write this story before I get to it. When you are done reading this story you will not say, "That is the exact same thing that happened to me when I was a kid." This will be a Richard Edward Noble classic.

My mother liked to knit and crochet. Whenever she had a free moment she was putting fringe on a handkerchief, knitting or crocheting hats, mittens, afghans or whatever. We had decorative doilies on the arms and headpiece of every chair in the living room. Her only outlet for most of this stuff was Christmas time – she dumped them onto my little cousins and my aunts and uncles.

But, in my mother's defense, I must say that her handcrafted items were usable. Unlike that pair of cufflinks and matching tie clip that floated around the family for about 14 years. I think I got those genuine, solid stone, maroon cuff links and matching stone tie clip six different times.

I gave them to my Uncle Vinnie the first time. What sweet revenge it was to watch his face when I gave them to him once again about six Christmas transfers later.

When I got them back the first time, I remember how shocked I was. How could anybody recycle a Christmas gift? I ran and showed them to my mother. "These are the ones I gave to Uncle Vinnie two Christmases past," I complained. She laughed. When she gave them to me to wrap for a new victim, I immediately wrote Uncle Vinnie's name on the card. My mother said, "You can't do that."

I said, "Watch me." She laughed again.

When Uncle Vinnie opened that box and saw those cufflinks and matching tie clip, his little smirk of a smile vanished. He looked at me. I beamed, a little angel waiting to be stroked.

"Well thank-you very much, Richie. These are just what I needed." Sure they are. You'll need to palm them off on some other sucker next Christmas.

Little did I realize that rotating Christmas gifts was an ancient tradition.

But when it came to my mother's crocheted and knitted hats, scarves, mittens, doilies and whatever everyone was bubbling with praise. My mother felt that their praise was sincere. I always felt that what they were really saying was, "God Mary, when are you ever going to have enough money to buy a real present. This knitted crap is getting rather old, ain't it?"

In any case, to make a long story even longer, my mother decided that the praise from the relatives each Christmas was sufficient to send her little waif, Richie, off into the streets periodically carrying a cardboard suitcase full of her handicrafts, to be displayed as for profit items before neighbors on their doorstep.

Oh my god! The humiliation! I couldn't believe on that first occasion that she was actually serious. When I laughed at the ridiculousness of the idea she made such a big deal out of it, day after day, that I finally relented. Besides the fact that I was still too small and she was too big for me to take on mano a mano.

It was about two weeks before Christmas on that first occasion. It was early afternoon and it was flurrying. I had my stupid cardboard suitcase and she forced one of her dumb hats onto my head as an ad – it was alternating rows of red, white and blue with a pom-pom and some little Christmas bells on top. I tried to walk without bouncing.

    I couldn't just walk around the block and mosey on home because I knew she would grill me when I got back. What houses did you go to? What did the lady look like? What kind of furniture was in the apartment? I had to go to at least one real home.

    I walked around and around and around. I wanted to pick a nice house – one with nice people inside. I didn't want anybody yelling at me. I didn't want to meet any girls from my school class. Can you imagine?

    I found a nice looking home about two blocks away. The tenement was painted well – no pealing, scabby spots and no bubbles or rotten siding or steps. It was cream with dark brown trim. It had a big, open front porch. There were Christmas lights in all the windows and a pretty tree in a corner with a window on each side. It was real Christmassy. A person couldn't have all that type display and then be mean and nasty. Of course, we had the same display at our house and we weren't all that friendly.

    I drudged up the steps. The hall door had a bell in it. We had the same thing on our hall door. It looked like a roller-skate key or the doohickey on the back of a windup toy. You rotated it clockwise and it rattled – almost like a bell but not really. I rattled it. An old lady came to the window and peeked at me. I didn't look at her. I pretended I didn't see her. I rattled again. I heard her open the kitchen door down the hall. Then clomp, clomp, clomp down the hallway. I couldn't stand the thought of facing the lady eye to eye. So I opened my cardboard case and held the lid up in front of my face thus displaying the dumb crocheted hats in the stupid box but not my head and face.

The old woman opened the door, saw all the hats in my cardboard box and screeched. I didn't know whether to run or what. What the heck was she screeching about? Was there a rat in the box, a dirty pair of underwear ... what?

"Oh look at all the beautiful hats," she said.

Is she kidding me, I thought. I lowered my cardboard box, display suitcase slightly – just enough so that I could peek up at the lady.

"Did you make these hats?" she queried joyously.

(Yeah right, I knit hats instead of playing baseball? Give me some slack will ya lady.)

"No ma'am my mother did."

"Nancy! Come here and hurry." Oh no, Nancy was an eighth grade girl from St. Rita's. I recognized her. Maybe me being a little runt she never paid attention to me. Hopefully she wouldn't recognize me.

"Oh I know you," she said. "You're Carol's little brother." She was in the same class with my older sister. Great!

The old looking broad and her daughter or granddaughter were so thrilled with all the hats that they called in all the neighbors. Of course they all had daughters who went to St. Rita's too. I was totally humiliated. I was a glowing, flaming red. I thought I was going to have a nose bleed.

They wanted to buy all the hats. All the girls were putting them on and running to a mirror. My mother told me to get at least 50 cents each. I told the first lady who wanted a hat that the price was 50 cents and she said, "No, no ... here's a dollar." By the time I left the apartment I had sold one hat for as much as $3.50. I returned back to the house with an empty cardboard box full of money. My mother went nuts.

The good part of this story is that everybody was happy. I saw all the girls wearing my mother's hats at school everyday and they didn't bother me – no pinching cheeks or coochee, coochee baby talk.

The bad part of the story was that my mother then wanted me to go out every night before every Christmas selling hats – she had a ton of them. She had them under her bed, in the closet – everywhere. What had she ever planned to do with all those stupid hats?

I pulled a Tom Sawyer on some of my buddies. I told them that selling my mother's stupid hats was great fun and if they came with me I would give them some money. But the first time we got a door shut in our faces, they were gone. So there I was every Christmas, poor little Tiny Tim or Rickety Richard out in the cold and snow, selling crocheted hats door to door. My mother finally let me stop when I started sporting a four o'clock shadow. Cute is only cute on little people.

Dirty Dancing

Down in the catacombs of St. Rita's grammar school, between the little boy's room and the little girl's room there was an open area which was used for many different things. I think it served, primarily, as an eating area for the kids who rode the bus to school and who couldn't go home for lunch. But my greatest recollection was its use as a dance floor. The good nuns were the chaperones and the janitor, Mr. Bill Fitzgibbons was the DJ.

Now why the good nuns were indoctrinating all us little angels into the perils of the "Dance Hall" mentality was, to say the least, suspicious. I just didn't get it. Mr. Fitzgibbons needed a job and was getting paid, so what could the poor man do but go along with the ladies in black. [I would like to point out that the good nuns, the brothers and the priests were dressed in black, long before Johnny Cash came along Cash-ing in on the idea.]

There were all these nuns standing up in front of me in their super protective, multi-layered, suits of black armor on a day-in and day-out basis – everything female in their natures being covered from head to toe in black. Of course, I knew why. They were ashamed, and rightfully so. After all, how many times had we all been told the story of Adam and Eve?

It was a simple enough story to understand. There was Adam, happy as a lark up in the Garden of Eden.

Everything was okeydokey until you-know-who came along and then everything went to hell. Clearly the whole mess was the fault of Eve who lured poor, innocent Adam into sin – and we all know how she did it, don't we?

This lesson was very clear to me. Just take a look around the neighborhood. There was a barroom on every corner. And who filled these barrooms – not women … men, of course. They had all fallen for the tricks of their individual Eves and now look at them. They were miserable and piling into barrooms to drown their sorrows.

Look at my own house! My dad had fallen for my mother's tricks and now look at him! My god, could the story of Adam and Eve be any clearer?

In the light of such revelation why on earth would the good nuns be encouraging young innocent boys to get up close and personal to a bunch of little corrupting Eves? This was insanity … or was it?

Well, maybe not. Under all those heavy penitent black gowns there was really another naked woman, wasn't there. Ah huh! Yes, it was all a part of *the plan* wasn't it?

Well, they can fool some of the people most of the time and most of the people some of the time but they weren't fooling Dickey boy any of the time. I was way ahead of them. While most of the other guys were out there sashaying around on the dance floor, getting sucked into the curse, I would be in the little boy's room smoking cigarettes and trying to develop cancer.

Beside this biblical house of horrors, I remember this experience being rather a tragedy for many of the little girls also. I didn't have to be all that sharp to notice that some of the little girls never got asked to dance. Old Bill and the good nuns tried everything. They even had a dance where the girls were allowed to go and ask one of the boys. During these dances, the little boy's room was mobbed with more future cancer victims.

The biggest tragedy that I remember was the throw-a-shoe-out-onto-the-floor dance. I'll never forget this one little girl. She had a bad case of acne. My brother had a similar problem so I knew how serious a problem it could be. Every boy did his best to avoid picking up the little acne girl's shoe. A friend of mine picked her shoe up by accident. When he realized who the shoe belonged to, we both ran into the little boy's room. Bill Fitzgibbons was sent into the bathroom to drag us out but before he came to get us we ditched the shoe.

Back out in the ballroom, we two clowns sat in our wooden folding chairs staring through the crowded dance floor at two little girls sitting on their wooden folding chairs across the hall. One of the little girls was holding one shoe in her lap. She had obviously retrieved her shoe from the center of the dance floor before it got lost in the shuffle.

She stared at me.

From the look on her face, I felt that I knew exactly what she wanted to do with that shoe.

The other little girl, the one with the acne problem, was sitting there trying to hide her shoeless foot behind the rung of her chair. She was looking down at the floor too ashamed to look at anybody.

I looked at *One Shoe* across the hall and then at my buddy Johnny. He wasn't looking at anybody. He mostly sat staring up at the ceiling.

"Johnny," I said. "There is a girl over there with only one shoe who keeps looking over here at you. Don't you think that you should go get her shoe and give it back to her?"

"Screw you," he said. "You were the one who made me run into the bathroom and hide it."

"I did not. I went to have a cigarette and you followed me. I didn't even know you had her shoe."

"You did too."

"I did not!"

After the shoe dance finally ended, the girl with only one shoe got up from her chair and one-shoed her way out of the dance hall. Johnny and I watched as she hobbled up and down, like Chester from *Gun Smoke*, to the little girl's room.

"She should take off her other shoe," I said. "Then maybe she wouldn't look so bad. It really looks weird for her to be walking around with only one shoe like that. What do you think?"

"Screw you," Johnny said.

"What? I ain't saying anything. I just think she looks dumb hopping around with just one shoe. Don't you? I wonder what her mother is going to think when she comes home with one clean sock and one dirty sock?"

I looked at Johnny.

He glared at me. I decided to shut up.

Another dance or two went by before the girl with one shoe returned to the ballroom. We both watched her as she limped along all the way from the doorway to her seat at the far end of the hall. It seemed to take her an awfully long time.

"God, it's like she's turning into a cripple. What's so hard about walking with one shoe? There are people in China who don't have any shoes – no socks either," I said, trying to make Johnny feel a little better.

Johnny jumped from his seat and headed for the boy's room. Cigarette break, I thought. Good idea, so I followed.

When I got to the bathroom door, Johnny came bursting out with the little girl's shoe in his hand. He pushed me aside, like I had done something. What was he mad at me for? I went to the ballroom door and watched.

He walked across the floor over to the girl with only one shoe. She saw him coming but kept looking down at the floor. When he got in front of her, he stuck the shoe under her nose. She took her shoe without looking up at him and put it on her foot. The bottom of her sock was really black. Then suddenly she looked up. She was pale and her eyes exhibited a sort of shock. Johnny had obviously said something to her.

She got up from her seat and walked to the center of the dance floor with Johnny following. Then she turned and the two of them started dancing.

Oh my god, I couldn't believe it. Giving the girl her shoe would have been atonement enough in my book. Johnny had completely flipped out. What had gotten into him?

Then it came to me. It was as clear as could be. Johnny had gotten sucked in. It was the old Eve with acne trick – Another Adam bites the dust.

Radio Days

It is difficult to believe that there is anybody still alive who was born before the advent of the TV. Well, here I am, the barely alive living proof – and what is even scarier, there are many more just like me still walking around out there – medicinally fed, partially decaying zombies of sorts.

Technically the above is not true. Not the part about the zombies, that is true – the other part, about the TV.

I got into a debate with a fellow a while back where I claimed that I was born before the invention of the TV. Research shows that I was wrong.

I was born in 1943 and the TV came much sooner. What is even worse, we might have to admit to the Russian claim that they invented the TV. Vladimir Zworykin came up with the Cathode Ray tube in 1929. Eventually Vladimir got to the U.S. and found a job with Westinghouse so maybe we can claim the invention of the TV via our immigration and naturalization policies.

But what is true is that in the early days of my upbringing in Lawrence, there was no TV in our living room. I don't remember the exact year that we bought our first TV but I do remember those days when a floor model radio was the big living room attraction. I don't remember any fireside chats by FDR but I do remember *Fibber*

McGee & Molly. I also remember *Blondie and Dagwood Bumstead* ... Oh Blonnnnnnndie.

Early radio actually plays very big in my memory bank – or to get up with the times, should I say, my hard drive. My older brother and I had a radio on a small table next to our bed.

I was put to bed rather early and I didn't like it one bit. I didn't like being in that dark bedroom all alone for one thing. The little light illuminating the radio dial was almost perfect. Add to that little radio light, a slight crack of light slivering through a slightly ajar bedroom door and it was almost safe in that cave. But best of all was the uproarious company of Amos 'n' Andy, Jack Benny, the Great Gildersleeve, Fred Allen, George Burns and Gracie Allen, Abbott and Costello, Ozzie and Harriet, Our Miss Brooks, Baby Snooks, and all via that little radio on our bedroom night table. And there was no extravagant monthly bill for the service. Today we pay a monthly service fee for our *advertising.* In the old days the advertising paid for the service; all one had to buy was the radio. Well, that's progress for you – or is it progress for them?

Then who could forget the great adventures of *Buck Rogers and his Space Cadets.* I can still easily conger up a picture of my toy Buck Roger's Ray Gun. It had a crank on the side. When you turned the crank it shot off rays/sparks – not real rays/sparks. More like a little colored red light in the barrel that turned on and off as one cranked the magic cranker. I suppose Buck Rogers was to us radio kids as *Stars Wars* or *Star Trek* is to many of today's younger crowd.

Then there was *Captain Midnight.* I sent for his secret decoder ring. I had to take it into the closet to see it glow. It glowed green. I don't remember how the decoder ring worked but the first message that I spelled out with my secret decoder ring was ... DRINK MORE OVALTINE.

I remember being very disappointed in the *secret* message. The secret messages that followed in the weeks to come weren't much better. This may be a slight exaggeration but I did not feel excited about this whole secret message business – I felt ... violated. Yes, yes ... that's the word I want. I was violated. As I grew older and my life went on, I was violated more frequently and much more often. Being violated has become so much of what I am today, I not only expect to be violated – I think I like it. Each time it happens my lack of faith in everything is reaffirmed. Today if I am not violated in any interrelationship with other people and society in general, I get very nervous. "What are these people up to and how are they planning to violate me down the road?" is my constant thought. It has become the challenge of my life.

L – A – V – A ... yes Lava soap. Lava was creamed sandpaper hardened with a pumice emulsifying agent. It scrapped the dirt from your hide. It was a MAN's soap. For tough guys who weren't afraid of a little blood as they scrubbed.

And who could ever forget that, Call ... for ... Philip ... More –raise. Or What'll ya have? ... Pabst Blue Ribbon ... What'll ya have? ... Pabst Blue Ribbon.

Yes, of course, there was *the Thin Man* out there solving crimes but what about *the Fat Man*?

"There he goes, into that drugstore. He's stepping on the scales. Weight: 239 pounds. Fortune: DANGER! Who is it? The Fat Man!"

Who knows? ... Only *the Shadow* knows.

I also liked *Sherlock Homes* ... "Elementary, my dear Dr. Watson." But *Charlie Chan* and his number 1,2,3,4 sons were really good too. "Ah so, and what you thinkiee 'bout dat, my number one son? Ah so ... you are very wise my number three son." I don't thinkiee Charlie had any daughters. I no remember daughter number one.

Anybody remember *the Goldbergs*? I can still hear Molly talking to the lady in the tenement across the way as she rolls out her wash – Yoo - who, Mrs. Goldburg!

How about *Judy Canova* or the *Camel Comedy Hour* with Jimmy Durante and Garry Moore? There was *the Colgate Comedy Hour* too. And how about Mr. woo woo, Ed Wynn or Luster Cream Shampoo and *Backstage Wife – Mary Noble*.

You would think that Mary Noble, *Backstage Wife* would have been a favorite in my home. But I don't ever remember the Mary Noble who lived with me at 32 Chelmsford St. ever listening to that show. It was too much of a stretch for our neighborhood, I guess.

But in any case ... Hen-ree, Henry Aldrich. My gosh, whatever happened to *Henry Aldrich*?

I don't know which frightened me more, *Lights Out* or *the Inner Sanctum*. That creaking door on *the Inner Sanctum* and that horrid, cynical laugh was terrifyingly thrilling.

Dick Tracy and *Boston Blackie* were good but *Gang Busters* with the rat-a-tat-tat of the machine gun and the intro by J. Edgar Hoover were really about as paranoiac as anything we have today – real good stuff.

But for my money nothing could beat *Superman*. How can we top a guy who could leap tall buildings in a single bound – even two bounds would have been good. He was also faster than a speeding bullet and able to stop a locomotive and bend steel with his bare hands. If that weren't enough for anybody, he could fly. You couldn't see him fly on the radio, but you could hear him whoosh off. And all the while in real life he was just a "*mild-mannered*" reporter for the Daily Planet. But give the guy access to a telephone booth and ...Wow!

Some people claim that radio was better for the development of the human brain than our present day TV. I really can't say. I spent very little time listening to the radio and trying to grow my brain. Truthfully, the vast majority of my play time was spent out in the streets and on the sidewalks playing games with other kids.

We scaled baseball cards up against the curb, shot marbles, kicked the can, and called – red rover, red rover, send pinhead right over. Hide-and-Seek was actually pretty big. I remember thinking that was really fun. Tag was a little silly – especially if you had only two playing – but it worked. Stooping tag was even trickier. The girls did a lot of jumping rope. Fire hydrant and parking meter leaping kept me busy while walking down Broadway to go to the Star Theater or Kenner's to get my Thom McAn shoes.

Catch, outs, stickball ... Simon Says could really get outrageous with the one-legged umbrella steps or the backward skipping frog steps. Dodgeball was popular.

Just walking from one buddy's house to another buddy's house could take up hours. Basketball, as we grew, was super. School was a big interruption to playing. They could have cut some of that school business but education is the cure, you know. But the more we try to cure it, the worse it seems to get. Seventy to eighty percent of young people will not graduate from college. So I guess it will be Wal-Mart and McDonald's that will be left with the burden of supplying the American Dream to future generations. By the way, what is the American dream? I've forgotten.

I don't know if we developed a lot of brain back in those radio days but we certainly burned up a lot of energy and had a lot of fun.

Jimmy and His Dog Tige

Jimmy was my good buddy Jack's older brother. I think Jimmy was only a year or so older than Jack. Jack wasn't much with words but Jimmy was even less. Jimmy didn't talk at all.

In his younger days Jimmy was always getting into fights. I think it would be safe to say that Jimmy as a kid had a hair trigger. He would go off sometimes and nobody could tell *how come*.

One day I beat Jimmy in a game of basketball in St. Rita's schoolyard. Jimmy grabbed me up by the front of my shirt and slammed me against the school building. I thought he was going to kill me. He was two or three years older than me and I was seriously confused as to what I had done.

He held me there with his fists wrapped up in my shirt and glared at me. His eyes were burning. I said, "What? What's wrong? What did I do, Jimmy?"

He dropped me and left the schoolyard without saying a word. Jack was there with me. I said, "Jack what's bugging him?"

Jack said, "Don't mind him. He just doesn't like losing."

As time went on, I watched Jimmy get into other skirmishes with more skilled basketball players. I told Jack, "You know, your brother shouldn't really play basketball if he is going to beat the crap out of everybody who beats him in a game of one on one – either that or he is going to have to get a lot better at basketball himself." Jack laughed.

I was always late for high school – well grammar school also. I was running through the parking lot passed Kennedy's pool and then along the fence that separated Central Catholic from the old city jail. I was huffing and puffing and rushing as fast as I could up the hill, when I heard a voice. "Hey Nobes! Nobes!" I turned and looked around and it was one of the inmates at the city jail calling me. Who the heck would I know that's in the city jail? It was Jimmy.

"Hey Jimmy, what the hell you doing in there?"

"Aw ... just some bullshit. Hey, do you have an extra cigarette?" I had a half a pack of Lucky's in my pocket. I said, "Here, take the whole pack."

"No, no," he said. "I'll just take two."

That's what always intrigued me about Jimmy. He had this philosophy going on in his head. He never took stuff. He was always fair – except if he lost. He laughed a lot – at nothing. He would just look at you and then laugh. I offered him the whole pack and he only took two. I insisted that he take them all but he would have none of it – a Jimmy principle of moral character.

When I got my first grown up, fulltime job at S. H. Brennan's Meat Packing, Jimmy was working there. He taught me how to drive the truck and helped me learn all the routes. After work we would go have a few beers together.

Having a few beers with Jimmy was an experience. As I have said, he didn't talk. We would sit at the bar and stare into the mirror on the wall. Jimmy would look in the mirror and see me looking at him in the glass and he would laugh. "Want to go to Tubby Clark's," he'd ask.

"Sure."

Spending an evening drinking with Jimmy was an evening of thought and contemplation. Kind of like having a dog – or being a dog, I don't know which. "Hi, I'm Buster Brown. I live in a shoe. This is my dog Tige. He lives in there too." It was peculiar but after a while I got used to it.

The basic idea was to keep moving. I never knew what Jimmy was looking for but when we didn't find it at one place we went to another. Periodically during the evening he would look at me and then laugh. I'd say, "Something funny about my face or what?"

He'd say, "Let's go to the Arlington Club." So off we'd go – bar hopping. Jimmy was restless. I was happy to have company – words or no words.

I would see Jack and I'd say, "Went bar hopping with your brother last night."

"Oh really? What did he have to say?"

"What did he have to say? You mean Jimmy speaks? Does Jimmy talk to you?"

"Not really. But I can tell when he is screwed up or not. You know what I mean?"

"Not at all. I just sit there. I've got my own game going now. I try to beat him to the punch and suggest the next bar before he does."

"Are you winning?"

"No, but I've tied a couple of times."

Jimmy had this world going on in his mind and it was obviously funny and filled with principles – Jimmy principles.

We were off in Beverly somewhere. Jimmy was teaching me the North Shore truck delivery route for S.H. Brennan's Meat Packing. After two or three hours of silence he speaks, "Screw this, I've never gone this way before but this traffic is too much. I'm going to take a shortcut."

We wound around one tiny road after another. Jimmy was driving about 50 miles per hour in a 25 mile an hour zone. Our 12 or 13 foot high box, rail truck with 10 tons of swinging beef was bobbing and weaving. The truck felt as though we were riding on two wheels half the time.

We rounded a bend and then directly in front of us sat a railroad bridge. All Brennan drivers were warned about railroad bridges. They are low. They can rip the roof right off your truck. A driver had to be sure to know the height of his truck and the allowable height of the bridge. A warning sign was pasted to the dashboard of every truck along with the official height of the truck.

"Oh shit!" said Jimmy and he jammed on the brakes. We slowed down to a crawl. There was a dip in the road running under the railroad bridge. From where we were the bridge appeared to be about four feet below the level of our front bumper. "Do you think we can make it under that bridge?"

"Are you crazy? Not a chance. You will not only rip the top of this truck off but it looks to me that bridge is low enough to rip both of our heads off too. You better stop and back up."

"Screw it! I'm going for it." And Jimmy hit the gas. The truck leaped forward then dipped down the hill before the bridge. I hit the floor and braced myself for the impact. Zip ... we came out on the other side with no problem.

I unfolded my arms from around my head and looked up from the floor of the truck at Jimmy. He laughed.

We were off to the Marblehead Store. This store got ten or twelve cattle – in quarters. That meant each piece weighted about 200 pounds and we had to carry every piece about ten miles to get it to the back door of the meat market.

Backing in was another story. There was a small alley almost as wide as the truck – well maybe slightly wider. On one side of the alley was a package store and on the other side was a gift shop. Jimmy immediately started laughing.

"Want me to get out and direct you in?" I asked.

"No, not really. I'll get us some help."

Bamb, bamb! Jimmy bounces off one wall and then the other as he attempted to back into the alley. The guy from the package store was out in the street in nothing flat and then the lady from the gift store appeared for the opposing team. They each started giving directions. The lady signaled with her hands and screamed, "More the other way!" Bamb! We're bouncing off the package store wall.

The package store guy yells, "No, no, the other way!" Bamb bamb! We're bouncing off the gift shop wall. Jimmy has his serious face on like he is really trying not to hit anything. I'm shaking my head. I've seen Jimmy back down a winding, impossible alley in Boston and then between two other trucks with barely an inch to spare and not ever hit anything. He's busting balls – or whiskey bottles and tea cups. He looked at the lady, "That way?" he pantomimed, questioningly from behind the wheel of the truck.

"Yes, yes!" she screamed, nodding her head up and down in anxious agreement. "That way!"

"No no," screamed the package store guy. "The other F'in way you moron. Where did you get your license, Sears and Roebucks?"

Oops, package store guy loses. Bamb bamb!

The tail end of our truck finally hit the loading ramp. Now Jimmy was really going to hear about it, I figured. He was going to have to pass right by the two store owners to get around the corner to the meat market entrance.

But wait a minute. I tried to open my door. The walls were so close that the doors don't open. Jimmy rolled down his window, scootched out through the window and then slithered up onto the roof of the cab. Naturally my window is busted and won't roll down – as if Jimmy didn't know that. I must bungle over all the Dixie cups and tonic bottles to the driver's side of the cab, then scooch out the window and up onto the roof of the cab behind Jimmy. From the cab roof we climb onto the refrigeration compressor unit to the roof of the box truck. It is then, over the roof, hang from the back of the box by the fingertips and drop to the platform below. Upon landing Jimmy looked at me and after a slight pause, laughed.

"You really think that is F'n funny, don't you?"

And every time we returned to the Marblehead store Jimmy did the same thing. On one occasion he had this big heavy kid with him as a helper. The kid weighed over 250 pounds. The poor boy almost had a heart attack, I was told – and that was just going under the railroad bridge, never mind squeezing out the window and climbing up and over the truck.

I thought of Jimmy as a mental challenge. I was, like the *Jimmy Whisperer*. I had to learn the secret *Jimmy language*. Jimmy was uncontrollable, non-communicative, unpredictable, secretive and explosive but once you got into his style he could be very funny – in a dangerous sort of way.

I always liked traveling with him. It was quiet but intriguing. It was a way for me to get off by myself but yet not be alone.

Martha, the Preacher's Daughter

It is well documented throughout the annals of history that preacher's daughters are often problematic for their fathers. I don't know why this is so universally accepted but this phenomenon is not much debated – except by preachers. I know that many of my male friends have felt extremely blessed in having the good fortune as to have bumped into a preacher's daughter, here and there, while diligently trying to traverse their difficult years – assuaging "that hard to be governed passion of youth" as Ben Franklin so aptly testified. Ben went on to state that he felt himself lucky to not have caught *distemper* or something even worse. Yes, yes how often I have heard my contemporaries whisper the very same ejaculation.

In most areas a preacher's daughter usually accepts the direction laid before her by her father's testimony. It is only in certain areas that they most often have disagreement.

Martha was her father's daughter in 99% of his teachings. Her only real conflict came in dealing with the personal anxieties of young men while discussing life in the back seat of a '54 Ford or a '57 Chevy at a drive-in movie or other acceptable, popular locations.

In these situations her religious fervor was often dissipated by the persistence of a young man not so versed in the scriptures or moral philosophy. Martha was known to be a girl of few words and definite action. This was considered a good thing, if not a sure thing by most of the young men in the area.

But in this tale I am not going to get into those few areas where Martha disagreed with her daddy but rather I have chosen to discuss some of those areas where her faith and trust in the positions of her father were not lacking — automobile radiators for example.

A young friend of mine became extremely infatuated with Martha and certain of her many charms. He had convinced himself that her religious hang-ups were of minor significance and could be handled without much difficulty. For example, one could simply agree — until the lights went out and the movie started or whatever. My friend was doing quite well in this regard even to the point where he accepted her challenge to meet her father ... at their home ... adjacent to the church. This was worrisome to my pal.

"I don't know," he said. "This is kind of like making an appointment with God. I am supposed to go there, before God, and pretend that I am not screwing his daughter. And she is going to be standing there beside me pretending to be *unscrewed* herself. I don't know. I'm worried," he told me.

"Well first of all," I said. "This guy is not God. He is just a preacher. He might be on a little better terms with God than you are but he ain't going to know what is going on between you and Martha unless you give yourself away. Certainly Martha ain't going to say anything ... will she?"

"I don't know. She would have to be crazy to do that ... wouldn't she?"

"I would think so. I would guess that you won't have any problem."

So the two of them met with God the father and there was no problem. In fact, after the meeting Martha asked Dad if she could borrow the car so that her and her new pal could go for a drive to the beach for a little fun in the sun. Dad smiled benignly and handed her the keys.

God the father's car was a 59 Cadillac, fins and all ... red and cream colored. It was heavenly. Martha drove. Martha was very excited about this whole business ... extremely excited. When they finally pulled the heavenly chariot to the shore's edge, Martha was sitting on the edge of rationality. She turned off the ignition and wanted to play *submarine* and take the ship under right there in the front seat of God the father's 1959 red and cream with matching interior Cadillac car. My buddy absolutely and categorically refused. He felt that this would definitely be in the area of sacrilege or heresy and could be subject to burning at the stake or disemboweling at the least. In consequence, they rushed to the beach and discussed the nature of abstinence between two snuggly beach blankets. Their argument went back and forth and up and down but finally climaxed in a mutual agreement – two or three times.

The first portion of the ride home was very pleasant and relaxing but at about half the distance to home base, my pal noticed that the heat gauge on the Caddy was rising rather rapidly. He didn't say anything until it entered the danger zone.

"Martha, the temperature gauge is getting over to hot."

"It will be all right," said Martha.

A few more miles down the road and the temperature gauge was looking serious.

"Martha, stop at the next gas station."

"Why? We have plenty of gas," said Martha.

"It is not the gas that I am worried about. It's the temperature gauge. The car is overheating. We have got to stop and put some water in the radiator."

"I have never had to do that before. Maybe the gauge is coo-coo. I wouldn't worry about it."

My friend was very nervous.

"Martha, we better pull over and let this thing cool down. I think I see smoke coming out from under the hood. There is something wrong with the radiator."

"That is ridiculous. I have never had a problem with the radiator. Daddy always has the car checked and serviced. My father wouldn't let me use the car if there was something wrong with it."

"I am sure that your daddy didn't know that there was something wrong with it when he gave it to us. But there is something wrong now."

"I don't think that there is anything wrong."

"Yeah, well I do."

"I'll tell you what; let's pray on it. I am sure that God will help and protect us. Repeat after me ... Oh Lord, my God..."

"Oh Lord, my God..."

"Please don't let anything be wrong with our radiator and allow us to get home safely."

"Martha, God is not a mechanic. Henry Ford invented the automobile not Jesus.[1] You have got to stop at the next gas station."

Martha didn't believe in stopping ... she believed in praying. She prayed aloud all the way home. Steam was pouring out from under the hood when they pulled into her drive. The temperature gauge was off the meter. When she shut off the ignition she turned to my buddy and smiled. "You see," she said. "Nothing happened and we are home safe ... oh ye of little faith."

"Give me the damn keys!" my buddy demanded.

He grabbed a blanket and ran to the front of the car. The hood was so hot he could hardly touch it. He got the hood up. Everything was hissing and pissing all over. He tried to remove the radiator cap. He turned it ever so

---

[1] I know Henry Ford did not invent the automobile. Please don't interrupt me when I'm trying to think.

slightly with his hand wrapped in the blanket and it exploded. He jumped away from the car and watched.

Suddenly there was God the father behind him.

"Jesus, Mary and Joseph ... have mercy. What in the name of all that is holy have you done?"

"We didn't do anything, Daddy. It exploded by itself.[2] We're so lucky. I prayed us all the way home. And look here we are both safe and sound."

"Get in the house Martha and go to your room."

"Why, Daddy? We..."

"NEVER MIND WHY! Just do as I say and NOW!"

Martha burst into tears and went running into the house.

"What is the matter with you?" God the father said to my pal. "You just sat there and let Martha blow up my new Cadillac?"

"I asked her to pull over or to go to a gas station, but she wouldn't. She said God would protect us. She prayed all the way home. I didn't know what to do. I couldn't tell her that God wouldn't help us. That's what she believes."

"I know what she believes, boy. I taught her everything she knows."

"Really?"

"Yes, really. But I let her go with you because you looked like you had a little damn common sense! WHAT'S WRONG WITH YOU? Are you an idiot? Don't you know that radiators need water? What am I supposed to do now?"

"Ahh ... don't worry about me, sir, I'll just walk home."

"You'll walk home, well isn't that wonderful. He's going to walk home," God the father said looking up toward the heavens. "'Don't worry about him,' he says ... 'he will just walk home.' Can you believe this Jesus?"[3]

---

[2] That's what she always said.
[3] Need I say, once again, that there was no response?

My pal backed his butt out of the drive as quickly and softly as was reasonable.

In discussing this story over the years me and my buddy have both agreed. One can pray all he wants, but God is still not going to fill anybody's radiator.

Kirby Vacuum Cleaner Salesman

*"I've got a lovely bunch of Kirbys
See them all standing in a row
Big ones, small ones
Some as big as your head..."*

I was in a backroom of a Kirby vacuum cleaner store on South Broadway with a room full of other unemployed loony-tunes singing songs from the Kirby Vacuum Cleaner Song Book.

I couldn't believe it. Was I actually doing this? Was the Kirby guy who owned this store serious? Was the Kirby vacuum cleaner company serious?

I had gone everywhere looking for a job in Lawrence but there was nothing. My Uncle Ray once told me that Lawrence was a boom or bust kind of a town. Obviously this was, once again, the bust side, showing its ugly face. There was one job listed down at the employment office. I had been there three weeks in a row and they had one job. There were hundreds of people, it seemed, gainfully employed at the Lawrence Employment Office and between the whole bunch of them, they had one job to offer the thousands of unemployed who came wandering in through their doors. It was collecting swill for a family who owned a pig farm in North Andover. I was desperate. I took the swill collecting job. I lasted three days.

Swill is disgusting – after learning about swill, garbage seemed a joy and a pleasure. I could bathe in garbage. Garbage is to swill as a fart is to diarrhea.

I would wander into somebody's back yard, flip the lid on their gallon swill depository bucket which was embedded into the ground, take one look at the ten million maggots and a tiny, unintended sniff of the contents and start puking. I puked at least ten times in the first two days. On the third day, I made it through the entire morning without puking by holding my breath and closing my eyes appropriately.

At noon I climbed into the front seat with Jethro, the second son of Heathrow, the pig farm owner. Jethro was eating a chopped ham salad sandwich. "How's it going today?" he asked. He had a mouthful of gooey ham salad, slouching about his open mouth. Little pieces of ham and mayo were dribbling down his chin. I looked at him and gagged. He laughed and consequently made visible the big glob of slop he was chewing and the goopey white bread stuck all over his teeth. I puked all over the floor of the cab. He said, "Don't worry about it. We're a little behind. We'll clean it up later."

At the next stop I climbed out of the cab without stepping in my puke and disappeared through a swill lady's back yard and headed towards freedom. I never saw Jethro again. I didn't even pick up my check for my first two days.

The next day I saw this ad in the newspaper. "Great opportunity for right type person," it threatened. "Self-starter," that was me. "Motivated, go getter, leader, good money, great future, willing to accept a challenge, needs to be friendly and must like people." Wow, that was me in a nutshell. I was skeptical though. This could be another Marine Corps ad. It gave no address, just a phone number. I called and made an appointment for an interview.

The place of the interview was a Kirby Vacuum Cleaner store. I had sold magazines as a teenager. Did not do well. But maybe this was a job selling to walk-in customers? Maybe I'd be working inside this store? What did I have to lose? I certainly know how to say no. I learned to do it as a little kid and I never forgot ... no ... NOOO, ... no no no. I was good at it. What's the problem?

Inside I met the owner. He was a very personable man. I spoke to him directly, "Can I really make some money selling Kirby vacuum cleaners?"

"I have made more money selling Kirby vacuum cleaners than I have ever made doing anything else. What have you got to lose? You've got no job and no money now. You might make something here, or you might not. But here, you at least have a chance"

Here it was, Pascal's wager in economic terms. This guy should have been a philosopher. I decided to give it a try.

First we had a super-salesmen instruction class. A couple of top notch salesmen gave us a crash course. They were really good and this Kirby Vacuum Cleaner was not just a vacuum cleaner. It was a super-duper machine revolution. A person could not only vacuum a carpet with it, they could clean and shampoo them too. You could wash and polish your floor with it; you could clean your mattress with it; you could polish your car with it; you could drill holes with it; you could sand and refinish a wood floor with it; you could unclog a backed up toilet with it; you could bust concrete and mix cement with it; you could pave a highway with it. It did everything. It had more attachments than a Rube Goldberg perpetual motion machine. To tell you the truth, I loved the darn thing. After the demonstration I could hardly restrain myself from buying one – good thing I was broke.

It was beautiful also. The chassis was all stainless steel. It had super-duper better-batter-beater rollers. They beat your carpet as they cleaned. The tubing was unbreakable.

You could club an intruder to death with any of the super-duper extra strength attachment pipes. This thing was a vacuum, a mini motor scooter and a home security system. You could ride it to work. It could attack and kill people. It was wonderful. I wanted one.

So there you go. If I wanted one and I had never vacuumed a carpet in my life, why wouldn't everybody in the world want one? If not the world, maybe just all of North Lawrence?

The next day I was in the boiler room drumming up potential sales. We had an unbelievable offer. If a potential customer would just agree to sit and watch a half hour demonstration of a *totally new, revolutionary household invention*, they would get absolutely free one whole case – that's 24 bottles – of America's favorite drink ... Coca Cola. How could you beat it?

Obviously there were more lonely people with nothing to do evenings than I would have ever believed. A free case of coke impressed the heck out of people.

"But, I can tell you right now buddy, I ain't buying nothing. I got no extra money. I'm just getting by as it is."

"You mean you can't use a FREE case of Coke?"

"Sure, I'll take a free case of Coke if you want to give me one. But I ain't buying anything."

"Okay! Is 6 o'clock tonight all right with you and the little woman?"

"Fine."

The first week I gave away about 300 dollars worth of Coke without selling one vacuum cleaner. I met all kinds of neat, poor people. I thought my family was poor. All around the neighborhood there were stacks and stacks of people that were worse off than me and my family. It felt great giving all these very grateful, poor folk a whole case of FREE coke. I loved it. This was a great job. Maybe one day I'll sell a vacuum cleaner too.

And everybody liked my demonstration. It was like being on stage and I was putting on my own play. Everybody ooh-ed and aah-ed – a few even applauded. They all said that one day if they ever came into any money – you know, like if some rich relative died and left them a fortune or that millionaire guy on the TV ever knocked on their door – they would definitely buy the *old lady one o' dem cleaners*. I made lots of new, nice friends – but no money.

At the end of the week the boss called me into the office. "Ah, you are giving away a hell of a lot of Coke. Right now you owe me over three hundred dollars."

"I owe you?"

"Well who do you think is going to pay for all this Coke you're giving away?"

"Ah ... Mr. Kirby?"

"Mr. Kirby's dead. He died a long time ago. I'm fronting you on this Coke until you make your first sale but you seem to be missing the point. If the potential customers don't buy a vacuum, they don't get a case of coke."

"But that ain't what you told me to tell them on the phone?"

"What are you, little Georgie Washington? That is just what you tell them to get your foot in the door. Once you're in, you sell them a vacuum or they get no Coke." He appeared a little angry.

Of course, what my boss was suggesting was unethical. He obviously didn't care but then he probably didn't have Sister Agnes in fourth grade at St. Rita's either.

My appointment list dropped appreciably. I stopped offering the case of Coke free. I told my potential customers if they could say yes to one important question concerning my demonstration before I left their apartment they would be entitled to a free case of Coke. Most folks on the phone declined my *just say yes* once in a lifetime offer.

Then I thought up a new idea. I would shampoo one room of carpeting for any couple who would sit through my half hour demonstration. One bottle of super-duper shampoo could clean a number of rugs. It was much cheaper than the free coke. Of course it involved my time – but what was I doing that I had to worry about my time?

By the end of the month, I was pretty good at shampooing rugs. I could do a whole living room in less than an hour. People liked getting a free rug shampoo but they certainly didn't want any super-duper carpet cleaner.

After a month or two I realized that I was never going to sell one of these darn vacuum cleaners to people in my neighborhood all of whom thought that $200 was an inheritance. But maybe I could use my demonstration model Kirby vacuum to make some money cleaning and shampooing people's carpets?

I charged twenty-five bucks for a living room rug. I made $150 the first week. By the end of the month I was able to pay off my Coca-Cola bill.

My Kirby sales career ended when during a demonstration, my cigarette rolled out of the ash tray I had resting next to me on the floor and burnt a tiny spot in the homeowner's rug. The lady was livid. I promised to remove the burnt mark with a super-duper free shampoo with our wonder Kirby stain removing shampoo.

I managed to snip the burnt spot out of her carpet with a pair of scissors when she wasn't looking and then shampoo over the area about a thousand times until the matting *grew* back together. When I was done I manipulated the coffee table a hair or two with one of the feet covering the hole. The lady inspected but couldn't find the spot where the burn had been.

I gave her a false name and a phony telephone number and told her to call if she found any problem. The hell with Sister Agnes, this ethics business was too expensive.

I turned in my demonstration model and resigned my commission as a certified Kirby Vacuum Cleaner salesman. But I would still love to own one of those Kirby vacuum cleaners. If I ever win the lottery or a jackpot in Biloxi, I'm going to get me one even if I don't have any carpeting. I won't hide it away in some closet, either. It is going to sit in the living room where everybody can see it. Call it conspicuous consumption if you want to, but a Kirby in the living room is as good as a Caddy in the trailer park. You better believe it!

Lennie's on the Turnpike

Being a jazz buff from early on, my favorite nightspot was Lennie's on the Turnpike. When all my friends were into the Beatles and Elvis, I was buying albums by Count Basie, Benny Goodman and Tommy and Jimmy Dorsey. I was listening to Peggy Lee, the Dave Brubeck Quartet, the Modern Jazz Quartet and Ella Fitzgerald when my contemporaries were listening to Janis Joplin, the Monkeys, the Beach Boys and the Dave Clark Five. My older brother Ernie got me hooked by introducing me to disk jockeys like Bill Marlowe on WILD – music spelled m–u–s–i–c not n-o-i-s-e – and late night Norm Nathan on WHDH with his *Sounds in the Night*.

Lennie's on the Turnpike was owned by Lennie Sogoloff. He was a record salesman for Columbia Records in his early days. The Route 1 turnpike was originally called the Newburyport turnpike and Lennie's club was technically located in Peabody. It was a tiny place sandwiched in between a trailer park and a truck rental. The inside was cramped and had low ceilings and small area tables. Herb Pomeroy's big band would blow you to another level – Buddy Rich and Woody Herman were even more dynamic. It was often asked of Lennie how he could afford to have these big bands at his tiny club. The band took up half the room. Linnie said that if there were ten or fifteen guys who could drink more booze than the Buddy Rich Band, let him know because he would hire them also.

Lennie started out in the nightclub business with Penny Abell at the Paddock Club in West Peabody. Lennie's, originally called the Turnpike Club, opened in 1951. Lennie bought Abell out in 1953. The club was destroyed by a fire in 1971 and Lennie then went to Danvers and opened the Village Green. Lennie donated all of his memorabilia to Salem State College. It is told that comedian Jay Leno got his start at Lennie's. He approached Lennie and asked if he ever thought of having a comedian warm up the crowd. Lennie auditioned Leno on the spot and hired him.

At Lennie's I saw many jazz greats perform. I saw pianist Theloneous Monk and a young drummer by the name of Allen Dawson. Alan was associated with Berklee College of Music in Boston and filling in on the drums at Lennie's in his free time. He would often appear with Illinois Jacquet and Milt Buckner. Buckner played the organ and Jacquet the sax. Those guys would go crazy. They were professional showmen as well as musicians. Dawson was the house drummer at Lennie's from 1963 to 1970. I was lucky enough to see and hear in person pianist Ahmad Jamal, the Modern Jazz Quartet featuring vibraphonist, Milt Jackson and bassist Ray Brown, Oscar Peterson and Miles Davis, Earl Fatha Hines, Rolland Kirk and his multiple horns and Kenny Burrell. Kenny like Dawson was just a young man and he often conducted matinee teach-ins or workshops for young aspiring guitarists. Dawson did the same for drummers.

I had an interesting experience on a trip out to route 1 to listen to Miles Davis one evening. On most evenings at Lennie's there was no door charge. I would get one of Lennie's famous roast beef sandwiches with a kosher dill pickle or the equally delicious corned beef on rye, buy a few beers and enjoy the music. On the night that Miles

Davis was appearing, there was a very large black dude collecting money at the entrance. This night there was an extreme 5 dollar door charge. In the past I had paid a dollar or two once in a while but never anything as outrageous as 5 dollars. But, of course, Miles Davis was a well known trumpeter even way back then. I had several Miles Davis albums at home. I was reluctant to pay 5 bucks but this was something special. Miles was considered an unusually gifted jazz talent.

After paying my five dollars and finding a seat, I ordered my sandwich and waited for the performance to begin. I sat through the first set listening to a very disturbing man at the bar rant, rave and laugh to the distraction of everyone. To compound this annoyance there was no Miles Davis. The Miles Davis sidemen were doing the entertaining.

Lennie, the owner, was a serious jazz music fan. I had been there many nights when he stepped to the microphone and asked the *tourists* who were not interested in the music to mosey on down the road. I admired Lennie for taking such a stand. But where was he on this evening?

The second set started and once again no Miles Davis and the disturbing man at the bar continued to act up. Finally I had enough. I headed for the door. I stopped at the bar and spoke to the manager.

"I am not happy," I told him. "I came here to listen to Miles Davis. I was even willing to pay the unusual five dollar charge at the door. I have been here for two sets and I have not heard Miles Davis yet. His backup group might have been entertaining enough if you quieted down the loudmouthed drunk over the other side of the bar who has been spoiling the whole show. I am very surprised to see, here at Lennie's of all places, that this is allowed to happen. You guys are usually Johnny-on-the-spot with these sorts of annoying clowns. What is going on here tonight? Is this the new Lennie's or what? Where the heck is Miles Davis and why don't you shut up that drunk over there."

The guy behind the bar pursed his lips and looked at me with obvious frustration. "That *disturbing drunk* over there is Miles Davis." He then shrugged his shoulders and walked away.

On the way out I went up to the giant, black bouncer who was still collecting money. "Excuse me," I said. "I gave you five dollars on the way in as a payment to listen to Miles Davis play his trumpet. Miles Davis didn't play. I would like my five dollars back."

 I suddenly found myself surrounded by several other black Miles Davis henchmen. I was very sure that the man holding my five dollars didn't need their help. The large black fellow holding my five dollars and many other five dollar contributions went on to explain that it was not under his authority to give any money back. He only made collections and was not in charge of refunds. I would have to discuss that with the management. I decided to go away. That was one of my wiser choices. I have made several worse choices in similar circumstances.

I stopped buying Miles Davis albums and didn't buy another for over thirty years. That was one of my bad decisions. Those albums from that period are now collector's items.

But on another occasion Peter Shaheen and I sat in the parking lot drinking beer and listening to the Stan Kenton band ... for free. That was worth more than the five bucks I lost on Miles. The place was mobbed and we couldn't get inside. So we decided to hang out in the dirt parking lot. The music was exploding from inside. It could be heard a mile away, I'm sure. There was even a waitress assigned to the parking area. It was a great night, me and Peter sitting on the hood of my car, drinking cold beer and listening to the Stan Kenton Band. We couldn't see the band or Stan but could we ever hear them. Fantastic!

Other than the Miles Davis experience, Lennie's on the Turnpike has been one of my fondest memories. If it weren't for Lennie's unique relationship with all these jazz superstars, I never would have had the opportunity to listen to any of those great musicians in person. It was quite an experience. I never ate Lennie's famous chili but I loved the roast beef on rye with the crunchy kosher dill pickle.

Barbershops

A lot of Italians owned barbershops in Lawrence. And it seemed that all the owners were named Guido. If the owner wasn't named Guido somebody working there was. Guido must mean something in Italian. Not something bad like mingya but something generic like *man who cuts hair* or bookie or some such thing.

I still don't know what mingya means, but, mingya, what does it matter? I called an old friend from Lawrence the other day and he said, "Mingya, Nobes, I haven't heard from you for forever. Mingya, this is great! What have you been up to?"

Nevertheless barbershops were multi-cultural in the Lawrence I grew up in.

I got my first haircut up on Center St. The barber was a friend of my Uncle Ray's. He was either Irish or English. I can't remember his last name but I can see him in my memory's eye quite clearly. I think his shop may have been called John's – John's Barbershop. It had the red, white and blue barber pole outside and everything. I remember being frightened to death and crying through the whole ordeal.

John had a special kid's seat that he placed onto the barber's chair. I cried and everybody else in the shop laughed, including my uncle. I didn't get it at the time.

I don't know why barbers scare little boys but I witnessed the same scene over and over as my life continued. I don't mean that I continued crying every time I got a haircut as I grew older but I watched as other young fathers brought in their little boys for the frightening experience. As an adult I laughed and chuckled with everybody else. It was one of those *been there, done that* type things. The kids always cried. I don't ever remember seeing a happy little boy sitting in a barber's chair his first time out.

Before this guy, my mother would put a soup bowl on the top of my head and cut around it. I was never overly concerned with appearances but the barber on Center St. made me look a lot better than my mother and her soup bowl.

I went to John until I went into business for myself as an Eagle Tribune delivery boy. The first stop on my route was Joe Blazavitch's Barbershop on Park St. It was across the street from King Tut's drugstore.

Joe had twin daughters, as I remember. They were very pretty and had extra long, shiny, brown hair. They were both in my class at St. Rita's but that fact did not intimidate me. I made the big decision to switch barbers and start going to Joe.

Changing barbers was a big decision. I think it had something to do with the nature of human bonding. I don't know the details but I can tell you it was difficult to walk past John's Barbershop after I switched to Joe.

I decided to go to Joe Blazavitch's Barbershop not because he had two pretty daughters who were in the same class as me at St. Rita's grammar school but because, I was now a businessman as was Joe. I felt that us local businessmen had to stick together. Joe bought my newspapers, so Joe was the man to cut my hair. It was a business decision. It was nothing against you John – if you are still out there. You were good John and did a great job, but business is business. I hope you understand.

I went to Joe Blazavitch's barbershop from age eleven and a half until I was twenty-seven ... and a half. Joe was my main haircut man from then on.

Joe was a very nice man and he liked me. He kept asking me to join his barbershop quartet. I resisted on the flimsy grounds that I wasn't a barber. Joe said that being a barber was not a real requirement for being a member of a barbershop quartet. I didn't see how that could be possible. "But I can't sing," I told him. He made me sing the scale while I was sitting in his barber chair.

"Doe, rae, me, fa, so, la, tee, doe." My voice cracked on the second doe. "See, I told you I can't sing."

"Whataya talkin' about! That was great. You're a tenor. You'll be perfect."

I never joined. I wish I did. I'll bet it would have been fun.

As time went on Joe's barbershop went downhill. I don't know what happened to Joe's business. It might have been the Beatles and the long hair craze. Eventually, he only cut hair by appointment and he moved his shop off Park St. He went from a 3 or 4 seater to a 2 seater.

Me and Jack Greco were two of his regular appointments. We meet Joe at his new shop to get our haircut for Jack's wedding. Joe wouldn't take any money and he gave us both a hot shave for free. That was my first and my last hot shave.

Joe would never take a tip either. I think a haircut at the end of Joe's career was $2.00. When I first started at age 11, I think it was a quarter — but that seems impossible.

I couldn't figure why Joe would interrupt his evening to run down to his barbershop and cut my hair for a lousy two bucks. It seemed crazy. But he liked doing it, I could tell. I guess since he had been cutting my hair since I was eleven years old, he figured that it was his responsibility.

I think he got a good job working at Raytheon or Western Electric or Avco or something. It wasn't that he needed my two bucks. It could have been that barbering was his love and Avco was his job. No one has ever heard of an *Avco Quartet* after all.

When Joe finally hung up the old clippers, I had a hell of a time finding a new barber. I started going to this Italian guy ... Guido, of course. But a haircut at Guido's took too long. The phone kept ringing and Guido would rush off to the backroom. People kept running in and giving him quarters after which he had to write their number down on a piece of scratch paper. He had the racing program in his back pocket. Guys would come into the shop, Guido would hand them the program and they would sit and make their picks. Then he was constantly pulling out that big roll of small bills and making change for his non-haircut customers. Guido had a very good business but it wasn't cutting hair.

The next barber I found was good – but he was very, very old. His shop was up on Lawrence St. His hands shook like crazy. He would have to rush the clippers to my head to get his hand to stop shaking. When he got to the shaving cream and the razor part it got real scary.

At first I thought the old buck was just nervous, but he wasn't. He just had the shakes. I felt sorry for him. But when the conflict in a relationship comes to frightened or sorry, frightened always wins.

I read about a brain surgeon recently who developed a case of the shakes. His insurance company denied his claim that having the shakes was bad for his type business. As far as I know the insurance company won their case. I think if I were that surgeon, I would be appealing that decision.

I bounced from one problematic barber to another for a number of years. Then at long last I met Carol. I kept moaning and groaning about my 10 and 12 dollar haircuts and finally she volunteered. I asked if she used a bowl. She said no bowl. Carol has been my barber for about 35 years now. I owe her a lot of money. I feel bad about that fact. But, when it comes to a choice between money and feeling bad, I usually opt for feeling bad.

Barrooms

Lawrence had a wealth of churches – some really beautiful churches too. I remember how shocked I was when I learned that the Immaculate Conception Church had been torn down. Some very famous people had been married in that church – my buddy Jack Greco for example. I was his best man. That alone should have been reason enough for preservation. I didn't think that it was allowed to destroy a church – especially a Catholic church – and a Catholic church in Lawrence. Where is that pope when you really need him!

Lawrence had its eateries, diners, bakeries and mills. But the one thing that may have outnumbered all of these landmarks was barrooms. Barrooms, taverns and nightclubs were everywhere.

I worked at S. H. Brennan Meat Packing on Broadway. It was a door or two down from Essex St.

Speaking of Essex and Broadway, what happened to the post office? Man if that building had been down here in the South it would be a shrine. They save any building that was built before 1860 down here. I told the mayor here that my whole hometown of Lawrence, Massachusetts was built before 1860. He wanted to know why, if I liked that town so much, I ever left. The mayor is, of course, a local who has a bumper sticker that reads: We don't give a damn how you did it up North.

I remember parking my truck at the dealership across from Brennan's. Some days I would work from 5 or 6 in the morning until 8 or 9 at night. It would be too late to go home and change clothes and catch one of my buddies for a night out on the town. So I would just walk home.

One night instead of just passing by all the bars on my way up Broadway, I decided to try an experiment. I would have one beer in every bar I passed on the way home. A beer was a dime in those days.

First I went around the corner to Al's Tavern and then into Tubby Clark's for a quickie and fortify myself for the challenge. I don't think I got four doors up Broadway before I hit another joint. It was an Irish place – O'Toole's or some such thing.

There were more barrooms on Broadway than I had estimated. I can't give you all the names but there were a few Builder and Trade Clubs and a plethora of other significant craft type joints. There was a place called the Flamingo. There was also a place with a piano bar, the Wonder Bar. There was an entertainer there who was a one man phenomenon. His name was Walter Reich. He played all the instruments and pre-recorded himself. He had a stage full of tape recorders and such. This was prior to the electronic boom and karaoke. It was something to just watch this guy coordinate all his tape recorders. He sang but didn't dance. He was good. He was definitely worth a dime.

I think I ended up at Cain and Bernard's 'round midnight.

By the time I left Cain and Bernard's and took a right onto Arlington St, I was singing at the top of my lungs such old favorites as: *Jingle Bells, Did Your Mother Come from Ireland, I'm Looking over a Four Leaf Clover* and *A Little Bit of Heaven*. You remember A Little Bit of Heaven – *So they sprinkled it with stardust just to make the shamrocks grow*.

On another occasion, I decided that Broadway was too dangerous for my one beer scientific experiment. I tried instead going up Essex St. to Lawrence St. and then through to Chelmsford.

That route was not much better. I bumped into Jimmy Sheehy on that occasion. I told him about my experiment and he liked the idea and joined me. As I remember we ended up sleeping in a parked car. He had the front seat and I took the back. When the owner of the car woke us in the morning we accused him of kidnapping us. We immediately checked our wallets and demanded that he return our money. He didn't call the police. So I guess our tactic worked. Actually he turned out to be an old buddy of Jimmy's and just laughed.

The Tally-ho, the Bamboo Room, the Merry Mac Club, the Polish National, the Irish Social, the English Social, the Capri, the Chez-When, there were a million places to drink, party and play games. At places like Cain and Bernard's or the Builders and Trades it was genealogy. Somebody would ask your name and off they went. "Are you any relation to the Noble girl who married Billy Callahan? Did your father marry a Dougherty?" In some of these bars the regulars knew more about you and your family than you did.

Shuffleboard and darts were big in those days. The bars sponsored intramural bar tournaments. Naturally we played for beers – another good excuse for getting sloshed.

The Tally-ho was the starting line for many of us each evening. After about four hours of warming up at the Tally-ho and who knows how many beers, it was off to the Merry Mac Club for the talent show, or to the Chez or the English Social for the strip show. The night would start at 6 and it wouldn't end until 1 or 2 in the morning.

In the morning I would be up at 5 a.m. and hiking down to Brennan's to unload a few sides of beef. My god! I don't know how I did it. If barhopping was an Olympic game, I think I could have won at least a silver medal. I would go for the gold but there were just too many extremely talented, professional drinkers in Lawrence for me to even fantasize about such a victory.

About 20 years ago I went back to Lawrence for an old gang from-the-street-corner reunion. After an outing at the park a bunch of the old gang ended up at Jack Sheehy's Pizza Pub on Lawrence St. There were ten or fifteen of us sitting along one wall reminiscing. A round of drinks consisted of 10 orange juice, 2 cranberry cocktails and four Virgin Mary's. Most of the old gang were active members of AA – that's not the automobile club, that's the AAA.

Evolution of Heat

Nobody that I hung-out with had air-conditioning or an air-conditioner in Lawrence when I was growing up, but heat was another story.

We had a coal bin down in the cellar. I can remember the coal truck pulling up to the house. It had a tin ramp or shoot that came down from the truck and fit into our cellar window. The coal was shoveled onto the ramp and slid down into the coal bin. There was a huge cloud of dust that filled the air. The man shoveling the coal was always black with soot from head to toe. In my pre-work preferences, being the coal delivery man appeared even less attractive than shoveling horse manure down at the city barn on Daisy St. A job vocation that always brought us kids a laugh. "You'll probably end up shoveling sh-t down at the city barn," was a common criticism.

I would go down into the cellar and with a shovel, fill a pail with coal. I was very small because I remember lifting the pail up the cellar steps one step at a time with both hands. The coal went into a compartment on the left side of our big, iron, wood-burning stove. The kitchen stove was the heat for the entire apartment. The back bedroom where my mom and dad slept would get so cold that ice would form on the *inside* of the two windows in the room. We had a black cat that would sleep occasionally in the coal bin for some reason. If he accidentally got into the apartment my mother would go nuts.

I vaguely recall a furnace with a boiler and radiator in the house. In my imagination, I have memories of shoveling coal into some kind of furnace. I know there were places around the city that had radiators. I remember them clanging and rattling and shooting off steam. But radiators in our apartment could be a fantasy on my part.

After the coal came kerosene. The kerosene was worse than the coal as far as I was concerned. I had to lug a three gallon can two blocks. It could have been a five gallon can. I know it was heavy. It took me quite a while to get back from Camden St. The kerosene store was between Camden and Tenney Streets. I got it at a gas station or auto repair shop.

The kerosene can had a spring metering device built into the cap. When I got the can home, it took two of us to jack it up and place it upside down into the metering well. I remember how it gurgled and bubbled as it filled the well.

After the kerosene came oil. My uncle who owned the tenement had two fifty gallon drums installed in the cellar. Now I only had to go down into the cellar with the can and heft it back up the cellar stairs. Eventually my Uncle Joe came and hooked up some copper tubing that came up through the kitchen floor and fed the oil directly into the stove's oil burners. The oil burners were round cylinders with circular cloth wicks wrapped inside. There were metal things with holes in them that slipped into a groove around the wicks. No more trips down to the cellar with that heavy fuel can for little Richard.

Next came gas. I presume it was natural gas. I don't know how they got it to the house. It must have been piped in alongside the sewer and waterlines. The gas burner had two circular iron burners – much the same as today's gas burners.

I remember sitting on the kitchen floor and helping my Uncle Joe convert our old, wood stove one more time.

When I left that apartment at age 27 that some old stove was still there. The old Frigidaire refrigerator with no freezer and the tiny ice cube tray compartment was still there also.

I'm getting old now and my sister is even older. She lives in San Diego and I live in Florida. We visit via telephone. In our last conversation we began reminiscing about the old days. We both remember vividly rushing to that old stove every cold winter morning. The first one up and out of bed got the best spot – right in front of the open oven door. The lucky individual who got up first would get to pull up a kitchen chair and sit in front of the open oven with his/her stocking feet up on the warm metal runner just bellow the oven. We always slept with our socks on – sometimes even a knitted or crotched hat to keep the heat in. My mother would tell me that the hat would keep the heat from escaping through the hole in my head. Very funny ... she thought.

As we talked about the past my sister commented on the tragedy of those days of poverty. She confessed her fear of ever being forced to live like that again. I sympathized with her but after hanging up, I reflected on her regret and fear. My life hadn't really changed all that much from those days. My wife and I had inhabited some rather rough living quarters in our thirty plus years together. The back of a Chevy van is one good example. We still sleep in winter with our socks on and wearing a hat to cover the obvious hole in our heads. I then told my wife that I really didn't feel as my sister did. "Those memories are some of my best memories. I don't get sad and cry when I think about them. I smile and laugh."

My wife looked at me curiously and then said, "That may be why we have lived the life we've lived."

Um? Maybe it is. I could just be a glutton for punishment I suppose.

Gambling

We were always gambling. Even as little guys sitting up the corner – tossing pennies, flipping coins, Forty-fives for a quarter on the game and a nickel up and down, or seven card stud, or clock, or draw poker, or mid-night baseball, or spit in the ocean, showdown, no-look poker, blackjack, even liar's poker. Expressions like: read 'em and weep, cards read, put up or shut up, you want to bet on it and you can't renege on the ace of hearts when the five is played, were a part of even our ten year old vocabulary.

Somebody always had a deck of Bicycle playing cards in their pocket. Eating, drinking and gambling were a Lawrence Unholy Trinity.

Why even the Church condoned gambling. I mean ... bingo? And then there were the card parties and the raffles? And they all had prizes to win. I don't know what the actual street value was for a case of Campbell's tomato soup or a ten pound Krakus brand canned ham but, hey ... it was all money in one shape or another.

As we got older different local ethnic entrepreneurs made a rather phenomenal discovery. They figured out that managing a gambling event could be a good business venture. Like all great ideas it struck a variety of different ethnic groups simultaneously. A few Syrian, Italian and Irish guys all stumbled onto this great idea almost in the same month it seems. It was kinda like McDonald's, Wendy's and Burger King. One day they weren't at all and then the next day, they were all everywhere. We had a giant, speculative poker bubble on our hands.

The idea was to rent an apartment for an evening or a weekend in a dumpy, non-descript area and host a poker party.

Now how one determined a dumpy apartment area in Lawrence was a *beauty is in the eye of the beholder* type thing. But truthfully, all us indigents knew a good area from a bad area, a bad street from a good street, even a questionable tenement from a legitimate tenement. We knew the safe streets and the streets to be avoided. If Mr. Samuel was invested heavily in the neighborhood, it was definitely questionable territory.

Samuel was the quintessential slumlord. He drove, unabashedly, his big new Cadillac from one dumpy tenement to another. Samuel was not alone. Other ethnics noted his success and there were soon a number of slumlords cruising about the city in their Cadillacs. Consequently there were plenty of optional locations for young gambling management hopefuls.

Somebody had discovered that by simply taking an ante out of each hand a profit could be made by the end of any given night. For example, when the ante was a quarter the house took one quarter. As the ante grew so did the house cut. Oftentimes by the end of a hot night of gambling the ante would have risen from a quarter to as much as five dollars.

There would be so many hands played that not only could rents be paid but snacks like pizzas, anchovy and sausage crispellis, beer and Italian meat pies could be supplied to participating guests free of charge.

I don't really know what happened but eventually the cops got involved in this thriving industry. Then, of course, price creep set in and the cost of hosting a party began escalating. Then over-zealous negative competition, the inevitable consequence of our capitalist society, raised its ugly head. Hosts began ratting to the cops on one another. This was followed by several *incidents*. Disgruntled customers began showing up with knives and revolvers and before you knew it another great, free market, business idea was biting the dust. More proof that free market capitalism is a spoof in the fable category. In the real world a managed capitalism, complete with payoffs and bonuses is the norm – with all prominent parties getting their appropriate cut.

I heard that the little guys got bumped by the bigger guys who could afford to buy off the cops and provide security but then the common crowd that was feeding the growth was priced out of the market. The local neighborhood thing had gone multi-neighborhood and then multi-gangster and the lucrative, speculative investment bubble was burst.

I have always heard that along with gambling came prostitution. I only remember meeting one alleged prostitute during my career in Lawrence.

Me and some of my buddies were in-between watering hole stops one evening and we decided to give our stomachs a coating of protective enzymes. We stopped at Bea's sandwich shop on Broadway just before closing time. As I stumbled through the front door, I noticed a young lady standing at the jukebox. She looked rather unique to me. I was always attracted by unique looking girls especially when I was drunk or almost drunk or just prior to passing out. I often had visions at that point – they bordered on the mystical or the beatific. On occasion I was blessed with the *Gift of Tongues* and I could speak in three different languages simultaneously. It was all rather miraculous.

She was snapping her fingers and jiving to some tunes wafting into the delicious smelling Bea's atmosphere. She was wearing a pair of black leather men's motorcycle boots with chains dangling from the upper rims. The boots ended half way up her calves and from there to slightly below her crotch, it was all skin. A little miniskirt was next, then more skin up to just below the boob area. The boobs were held sloppily yet suggestively in place by a stretchy halter top. The halter was an extremely tight fit.

This was December and it was snowing outside so naturally she was wearing her boot matching, insulated, black leather, motorcycle jacket. It also had several chains and a few colorful rabbit's feet here and there and a nifty skull and crossbones painted on the back.

Her lips were smeared with a thick coating of pasty, fire engine red lipstick. Her eye-shadow was dark purple which probably looked better when in a corner booth in a dark strip joint like the Chez-When at two or three in the morning. Her hair displayed a straw, kitchen broom-like texture and a burnt, orange-yellow color. She was clearly a Fazio beauty school alumnus.

She had a metal comb sticking out of her hand-carved and beaded, leather purse which had a beautiful Rolling Stone, Navaho guitar carrying strap. The metal comb had a long handle, the tip of which was sharpened to a razor's edge. Both of her arms were covered with multi-colored plastic bracelets that rattled as she jived and snapped her fingers. She probably worked part-time as a waitress or barmaid at Tubby's, the old Horse Shoe or the Brass Rail.

I took one look at her and it was love at first sight.

I immediately fell a few stumbles in her direction. "Hi there, what's a nice girl like you doing in a place like this?" I blubbered, sluringly. She was chewing gum and blowing a large bubble at that moment. After the bubble burst she spoke.

"Go screw yourself, you blank, *expletive*, blank blank."

"Oh come on now, what kinda talk is that coming from a sweet looking girl like you," I crooned, Smirnoff-like. "I'll bet you graduated from St. Mary's High didn't you?" She smiled coyly, revealing some interesting dental work obviously performed by a previous boyfriend.

"How did you know?" she said sarcastically while broadening her grin sheepishly and blowing another bubble with her gum.

"I could tell by the little gold crosses dangling from the chains on your motorcycle boots and the St. Christopher medal attached to some of your rabbit's feet."

She then popped up her middle finger and said, "Why don't you take your blank blank and stuff it up your blank."

"Well, all right! That sounds like sex talk to me," I exclaimed. "Let's get to it."

My buddies then grabbed me and pulled me off to the side. "Don't be messing with her." They whispered. "She a Pro."

"She plays golf?"

"Nooo stupid! She has sex with men for money."

"Really? Well, I'm game. How much does she pay?"

"She doesn't pay, you butthead. She collects."

I took another, longer and slower, look at the object of my new potential romantic involvement.

"No, I don't think that I am willing to accept that evaluation."

"It's true."

Well instead of my dream girl, I had a mushroom and green pepper cutlet and a cup of black coffee.

After two or three refills on the black coffee, things began to un-blur, solidify and take on a more actual, everyday congruity. I was still drunk but I was wide awake.

As we exited I said one last goodbye to my Bea's, jukebox queen Professional. She flashed me that crooked, well-worked smile then snapped me a double bird while blowing a Guinness Record achieving bubble with her mouthful of Bazooka bubble gum.

"You know," I said. "I don't know what I ever saw in you. You have been a huge disappointment. I'll never forget the way you've treated me this evening. And further more, I don't believe that you went to St. Mary's. I'll bet you graduated from Lawrence High."

She said, "Yeah, well take your blank and stuff it up your blank blank and when you are done with that go find yourself a great, big blank blank and suck on it."

"Wow," I said to my friends. "She really knows how to turn a guy on. Where do girls learn that sort of talk?"

"She was probably in the advanced class or the college program over at Lawrence High," one of my buddies offered.

"You don't think she went to St. Mary's?"

"No, I don't."

"Well then what's with all the gold crosses on her motorcycle boot chains and the St. Christopher medals on her rabbit's feet?"

"She's just into fancy jewelry."

"Yeah, I suppose you're right."

Hopping Cars

Hopping cars is what we called it. I don't know how it started or how we got the idea but it was a dandy.

Hopping cars was a wintertime sport and it required snow. There had to be a good amount of snow and it was better if it was packed down. Ice was O.K. but slush was bad. It was not an organized sport, but it was very sporting.

We would hide behind parked cars and as an auto passed we would scurry out and grab onto the bumper. Then the challenge was, how long could a child hang on and how far could he ski behind the vehicle before he had to release his hold on the bumper and go sliding along on his face.

Some auto operators, if they spotted you sneaking out from behind a parked car, would stop and make you get off. But there were others who thought it was funny.

We had one neighborhood clown, who was half adult and half moron, who would purposely slow down as he passed a group of stupid little kids like us to lure us onto his bumper. Of course, it always worked. Three or four of us would crouch down, like we were getting away with something and scoot out into the road and hook onto his bumper. Once the local moron knew he hooked us, he would tromp on the gas. His car would skid from one side of the road to the other as we all hung on for our lives.

Sometimes our feet would slip out from under us and then Murray the Moron would drag us to the next corner or stop sign. Sometimes we would let go of the bumper and go sliding across the road and into a snow bank – or a parked car. It wasn't a sport for the faint of heart.

Everybody who was old enough to drive a car knew what we were up to. The sensible ones watched and stopped if they felt one of us nitwits had made it to their bumper but we were pretty sneaky.

We could spend a whole afternoon hopping cars – and on the same street. We usually hopped a car going one way and then waited and caught another going the other way.

If you were able to ski behind a car for one complete block, that was pretty good – two blocks was phenomenal.

We did most of our car hopping on Center St. and its tributaries. It was somewhat dangerous to be hopping cars up on Lawrence St. You could get tumbled out in front of an oncoming car or dropped off and get crushed by a following car. You wanted to find a single car operating on a side street with not too much traffic. A ride up Willow St. or Exchange St. going towards the Howard Playground was good.

I remember one time Bobby Pappalardo lost one of his gloves. He fell off and his glove stuck to the guy's bumper.

Hopping cars bare-handed was rugged – too cold and a wet, bare hand could stick to a cold frosty bumper. But Bobby toughed out the afternoon one-handed. Then the two of us hopped this car several hours later and Bobby screamed, "Hey, there's my glove!" And sure enough, there it was stuck to the bumper just where he had left it earlier.

On another occasion we spotted this lady driver. We especially liked lady drivers. They didn't go too fast and they never stopped the car, ran around the back and booted any of us up the ass, like some of the male drivers were prone to do.

She was a younger lady, rather pretty and she was driving a little red Volkswagen. She was waiting at the corner of Exchange St. and Lawrence St. She lived up Birchwood Rd. We decided to hop a ride across Lawrence St. and then drop off halfway up the hill on Birchwood Rd. We crouched down and tucked in behind some parked cars. Just as the traffic cleared, about five of us scooted out and snuggled onto her bumper. She gave it the gas and off we did NOT go.

Exchange St. was on a slight incline at the top and with five of us hanging onto the bumper of that tiny Volkswagen, nobody was going anywhere.

The young lady couldn't figure out what was happening. After several attempts and the wheels just spinning in place, she put the emergency brake on and climbed out of the Bug. Us little morons were all still hanging there in a row. She looked down at us, put one hand on her hip and said, "Come on guys, how about giving a working girl a break." The jig was up. We didn't get a ride from the pretty young lady, but we did get to push her out of the little trenches she had dug for herself under each tire because of us.

I don't have to wonder if this little sport is still going on. I'm sure the kids in Lawrence are not any brighter than when I was there, but fortunately cars no longer have bumpers. I suppose there might be a pickup truck or two up there these days. It might still be possible.

Sewer Covers

Today's question is: Can a sewer cover be made to fall through the hole that it was designed to cover?

We were playing stickball up the old Howard Playstead when our sponge rubber ball got away from us. It rolled down the Birchwood Rd. hill or went over the Howard Corner wall and right into the sewer on Lawrence St.

Losing rubber balls of one type or another down a corner sewer was a common childhood experience in Lawrence and I imagine in any inner city. The balls were not all that expensive as I remember, but none of us ever had a dime between ten of us. Even if we all chipped in and came up with the required amount then we would have the problem of whom the ball actually belonged to once the game was concluded. But in truth the option of buying a new ball was rarely even considered.

We all gathered around the sewer and contemplated.

The ball was right there. We could see it bobbing up and down. Could we get it with a stick or maybe two sticks? What about a tree branch? How about a coat hanger with a loop in the bottom tied to the end of a stick? How about a stick with a Dixie Cup tacked to the end of it? This was a job for Plastic Man.

What if we lifted the sewer cover off the hole and then had the one of us with the longest arms reach down into the sewer and grab up our ball? Good idea.

The sewer cover was heavier than we thought. It took four of us gripping the sewer cover through the square holes to get it up and carry it off to the side. But then we realized that our sewer with no cover was right on the corner of busy Lawrence St. and Birchwood Rd. If a car was coming up Lawrence St. heading to Broadway and it wanted to turn on Birchwood, its front tire could go right into the hole. Oh man, it could get destroyed.

Some of us would have to direct traffic around the sewer hole while the rest of us rescued our ball.

Well ... not so simple! Even Dolan who was all arms couldn't reach it – even with one of us sitting on his calves while two of us each grabbed onto a foot and sneaker. There was only one way. We would have to dip Dolan down into the sewer, head first, while two of us held him by the legs.

Dolan opposed this idea. "What if you guys drop me?" he argued.

"Why would we drop you?" we countered.

"Because two of you ain't strong enough."

"Okay, what if we put two guys on each leg?"

"And what if you guys decide to drop me just for the fun of it?" Everybody laughed. "Yeah, see?"

"No we won't let you go. We need the ball. It would be stupid for us to let you go."

Dolan was not thoroughly convinced but he agreed. He laid down on the ground and scootched himself forward over the sewer hole as far as he could. Two of us on each side grabbed a leg and upsy-daizy went Dolan. We lowered him down into the sewer, head first.

It was a bit hairy there for a moment or two as proper positioning got a little cramped and guys started stumbling over one another's feet. Then Dolan, feeling the stumbling, began screaming and cursing up at us. Unfortunately this started me laughing. As the laughing spread, Dolan began screaming louder and louder. But in-between the sputtering we got him down low enough into the sewer that he was able to latch a mitt onto our ball. There were several other balls down there and one of the guys suggested to Dolan that while he was down there why didn't he toss the one he had in his hand up and out of the sewer and then start gathering up some of the others.

Dolan's response to this suggestion was not nice – very, very gutterish. A kind of sewer talk, you might say. This caused a resumption in the sputtering amongst the holding crew. Dolan demanded to be fished back up immediately.

We began stumbling away from the sewer in a direction to Dolan's advantage. When we finally dropped Dolan on the asphalt we all dropped to the ground laughing.

Okay, the operation was a success now all that was necessary was to get the cover back onto the sewer hole.

We took our positions around the sewer cover and dead-lifted the monster. We clumsily side-stepped, our way back to the sewer. We had four of us holding the sewer cover about 3 feet above the sewer hole. It was heavy and we were all straining. "Let's just drop it," someone suggested. "Then we can straighten it up."

It was agreed that on the count of three we would all let go of the sewer cover and jump backwards getting our toes out of the way. We didn't want any smushed toes.

"Okay ... one ... two ... three ... drop it!"

The drop went perfect and none of us got our toes smushed but to our total amazement the sewer cover dropped somewhat tilted and instead of landing a little off center, the damn thing went right through the hole and splashed down into the sewer.

For some reason our first reaction when any catastrophe struck, was to run. Somebody screamed "Oh shit!" and we all took off running. We didn't get further than the next corner when someone yelled, "We can't run away. What if a car goes into the sewer hole and then crashes and kills everybody?" We all spun around and ran back to the sewer hole. We positioned ourselves around the sewer and then sent Jack Greco, who lived nearby, to call the cops.

Calling the cops was not something that occurred to us on a regular basis. It fact, it almost never occurred to us. But on this occasion, it somehow came right to mind.

When the cops got there we told them that when we arrived at the corner to play a little stickball we noticed to our horror and shock that the sewer had no cover. So, good citizens that we were, we immediately stationed ourselves around the sewer and had somebody call the cops.

The cops looked at us very suspiciously but called the city department nevertheless. The city department came out with warning sawhorses with reflectors and placed them around the sewer. Both the cops and the city workers complimented us on our community spirit. One of the cops kept smirking at us as we all gleamed and glowed and took our bows. It was like he knew but for some reason wasn't going to rat on us. We all played it for all that it was worth. We were the little Howard Playground heroes.

But after the cops and everybody else left we all breathed a sigh of relief and slapped each other on the back. We agreed unanimously that removing the sewer cover was stupid. We tried to recall which one of us decided that we should all return to the scene of the crime and then have Grecs go back home and call the cops. Dolan said that it was his idea but that didn't ... float. We all quickly agreed that a good idea from Dolan would be without sufficient precedent.

It is rather amazing in retrospect to reflect on how *stupid* can turn into genius with the casual flip of a sewer cover.

Hangin' Out as Therapy

I left Lawrence at age twenty-seven. When I returned for an old corner gang reunion about twenty-five or thirty years later at the Pizza Pub on Lawrence St. (at present called the Celtic Club), I noticed that there were no corner gangs. I was told by my old corner gang buddies that they now had special police who infiltrated and broke up the corner gang syndrome. The old corner gang that was my salvation as a child had devolved into criminal organizations, I was told.

"The kids today don't just borrow a car and go for a joy ride like we used to do," my buddy Jack Sheehy informed me. "They steal a car, take it to a garage, break it down into its parts and sell it piece by piece and make a fortune."

"Umm, why didn't we think of that?"

"Because we were good kids and these kids today are gangsters, druggies and wackoes," offered a fellow from a nearby barstool.

"Not exactly," said Jack. "When we were kids all the parts of a car sold for a fraction of what a whole car sold for. If we took a car apart and sold it piece by piece, we would have been idiots. We probably never did it, because we couldn't make any money on it in those days."

"You know, that is a good question. Why didn't we get into more trouble than we did?"

"We weren't that smart," someone offered.

"But what about the smaller kids? Where do they all hang out these days? We hung out in the streets and on the corners as far back as I can remember."

"They go to camp."

"Yeah right! These tenement houses don't look any better than they did thirty years ago – if anything they look worse. They got welfare camps these days?"

And so the barroom chatter rolled on. I guess if the truth be known many kids got into trouble hanging out when we were kids too. Most of my old gang agrees that we were lucky. Drugs, big-time crime and extreme violence were not quite that fashionable in our corner days. I suppose we were lucky. I know, speaking for myself, it certainly had nothing to do with my innate intelligence. I feel that I am pretty smart today but most of what I learned came from doing everything wrong and realizing after the fact how stupid I'd been. That is called experience and it is learning the hard way.

But nevertheless, hanging out on the corner was for me the best part of everything that I remember about growing up in Lawrence. The buddies I made, the fun and laughs we had are the things I remember when I think positively about my childhood.

"Where you goin', son?"

"Up to the corner, Ma."

"What you goin' to be doin' up the corner?"

"Nothin'. Just goin' to hang out with my buddies."

It seems like I spent a lifetime standing on the corner *watching all the girls go by*. Yes, that was a part of it. We did a lot of that but mostly it was just hangin' out. It was companionship. It was shooting the breeze. It was airing frustrations. It was making one another laugh and teasing – a lot of teasing.

Guys and their girlfriends was another big problem. Often a guy would be so hurt and angry he would confess that he wanted to murder little Lulu or Nasty Nancy. I remember one of the old gang breaking up with his steady and then sitting up the corner planning her murder. We all listened positively. Finally he came up with the perfect plan; he would drown her in the surf at Salisbury beach.

"That is a good plan, Billy, but first you are going to have to take a few swimming lessons aren't you? You're the only guy I ever met who couldn't learn to float in salt water. I never saw anybody lay back in the salty surf at the beach and just sink to the bottom like you."

"I will drown her in the shallow water."

"Too many people will see you, man. You will never get away with it."

"I don't care if I get caught."

"Well, if you don't care if you get caught, why don't you just run her over with a car?"

"I don't have a car. I flunked the damn driver's license test again."

"Well how about pushing her off a curb into an oncoming Town Farm bus down on Essex St."

"Too many people watching ... and I hate the sight of blood."

"Oh, so that's why you like the drowning ... no blood huh?"

"Right."

"Why don't you poison her?"

"With what?"

"You know in Africa a tribe developed this poison called curare," offered Dutch who was always into the exotic. "They say it can't be traced. You could get a dart with some curare on it, then hide behind a tree with a blowgun and zap her as she is coming home from church or something."

"Not when she's coming home from church, man. You don't want to bring God into this."

"Right, I didn't think of that."

"Where the hell am I going to get some curare?"

"I don't know. But do you mean to tell us you have a blowgun?" I queried.

"No I don't have a blowgun. I don't even know how to work a blowgun."

"It's easy, just don't breathe in – blow out. Remember that; blow out ... no breathing in."

"You guys are a bunch of buttholes. Do you realize that?"

"Yeah right. Now remind us which one of us is devising a plan to kill his old girlfriend?"

"Well, she pissed me off!"

"Okay, so let's not give up so easy. Drowning is stupid for a guy who can't even float in the ocean. Pushing her in front of a Town Farm bus on Essex St. is too bloody. You don't have a blowgun? What else could you do? How about rat poison?"

"Yeah like she will eat a jar of rat poison."

"Well you don't just give her a jar of rat poison to eat. You put a bunch of rat poison into a Napoleon from Tripoli's Bakery. Everybody loves Napoleons."

"I like chocolate éclairs better," I offered.

"Did you ever have one of those things they sell down there with the cream stuff inside and the powdered sugar on top of a piecrust thing that is shaped like a giant sea shell?" Dutch asked.

"That's a lobster claw."

"I don't think so. It don't look like no lobster claw to me."

"Forget it. She don't eat any of that stuff. She is always on a damn diet. She eats stupid stuff made out of tree bark wrapped in oatmeal and sprinkled with wheat germ."

"Really, why would anybody eat anything that has germ as a part of its name?"

"I don't know, but that's the kind of stuff she eats. She takes a lot of pills though."

"Okay, that's it. Give her a poison vitamin pill."

"That's a great idea. Do they sell poison vitamin pills at Lawlor's Drug Store?"

"You know. You have no damn imagination. You just ought to forget about killing anybody – you don't have the brains for it."

"Oh right, thank-you Eddie Fisher – the Boston Strangler."

"Eddie Fisher wasn't the Boston Strangler."

"I know. He wasn't the real Boston Strangler. He was the guy who played the Boston Strangler in the movie."

"Eddie Fisher didn't play the Boston Strangler in the movies. It was that other guy, the one who played with Burt Lancaster and Gina Lola Bridgeda in *Trapeze*."

"That was Kirk Douglas."

"No, no, no. There was another guy. He had curly hair."

"Tony Curtis?"

"Yeah, that's the guy."

"How did we get to talking about Tony Curtis here? Let's get serious. How is Billy going to kill his girlfriend and not get caught?"

"He doesn't care if he gets caught."

"Well, that is just stupid. Why would you kill somebody and just let yourself get caught. That's sick, man."

"Billy, that's your problem … you're sick, man."

"You know, you guys are right. I am sick and I know how I got sick. I spend all my time sitting on this corner talking with you nitwits."

"That must be it. What do you guys think?"

"I think we all agree. We have driven Billy out of his mind and now that is why he is up here asking us to help him think of a way to kill his girlfriend. I think we all ought to be locked up. This is obviously a conspiracy. There is no doubt in my mind. It's us. Billy is fine. He had nothing to do with it. Case closed."

"You know I think that we ought to make an anomalous phone call to Billy's girlfriend and tell her that Billy is planning to kill her."

"There is no such word as anomalous. It's anonymous. And you guys better not call her!"

"Why not?"

"Because if you do, I'll kill you."

"Oh god, here we go again."

"I think anomalous is a word. It's got something to do with not being normal or something."

"Well, you should know."

The Frolics

The Frolics was a classy nightclub at Salisbury Beach. I think it was owned by the Mulcahy family. During the 50's when I was just a kid, the bulk of my knowledge of the Frolics was gained from peeking in the front door. I only went there once in the 60's. But it is still a big, big memory.

I was a jazz buff – and I remain so today. When all my drinking pals were going to the 5 O'clock Club and the Peppermint Lounge (Jenney's), I was sitting at the piano bar at the Normandy Club or across the street at the Kon-Tiki Lounge.

I lived at the 5 O'clock Club during the day with Bill, Harold, Helen and Maryanne. The evening kiddie action was at the 5 O'clock Club and Jenney's but the adult music was at the Normandy and the Kon Tiki. There was always something strange going on at the basement of the Edward's Hotel, but that's another story.

Bill Marlowe announced one afternoon on his radio show that Erroll Garner would be playing at the Frolics that evening. I had a big stack of Erroll Garner albums. I had a set of drums in my living room and I could swirl my brushes to Erroll Garner and his piano all day long. I could hardly believe that Erroll Garner would be coming to the Frolics.

The only friend that I had who also enjoyed jazz music was Peter Shaheen. He loved Frank Sinatra. He not only loved Frank but he could sing like him also and he often did, up at the old Merry Mac Club on Tuesday nights.

I ran to the phone and called Peter. I told him about Erroll being at the Frolics that evening. He was equally enthusiastic. I picked him up at his house. I lived on Chelmsford St. and he lived on the corner of Chelmsford and Center.

We decided to head up to the old Howard playground to see if any of the other guys were hangin' out. Maybe we could get a few more in the gang to go with us.

There was nobody there. We were about to head up the hill and off to the beach road when Paul Dobson came skidding around the corner in his mother's car. Paul had been borrowing his mother's car since the age of twelve. He was into leaving rubber while peeling out, speed shifting and skidding around corners. We all thought that Paul would end up drag racing at Indy or something. To everyone surprise, especially Walter of the infamous Walter's Variety store, Paul actually lived to become an old person. Every time Paul would skid around Walter's corner, Walter would groan … "On a slab. That kid will be on a slab one of these days."

"Hey Paul, you want to go see Erroll Garner at the Frolics?"

"Sure, I love Erroll Garner. He's one of my favorites!"

Paul skidded his mother's car back to the garage, jumped in with me and Peter and we were off.

"I didn't know that you liked Erroll Garner, Paul?" Peter asked.

"Oh man, I love him. What's the name of that hit song he sings?"

Peter and I looked at one another dubiously, "Erroll Garner don't sing, Paul. He's a jazz piano player."

"Oh yeah, that's right. But it's okay, I'll like whatever he does." Paul was pretty easy. I guess he just wanted to go somewhere.

We had an early winter setting in. It began to flurry as we headed to Salisbury via the 110 beach road through Haverhill. Of course we had to stop at the Merit Gas Station. Then it was out and off to the light and up passed that big, old, willow tree. We spent many an hour sitting under that giant willow tree. We thumbed to the beach all summer long as kids and for some reason we always got stuck in Haverhill and ended up weathering the drought sitting under that Willow tree.

We made it to the Frolics. There was about a quarter inch of snow on the road by the time we arrived. How we would get home, we didn't know and didn't care. We rushed up the long wooded steps to the Frolics and made a dash inside to make sure we got a good seat. To our surprise, the joint was still empty.

We sat at a table up front. We ordered our Hawaiian Coolers and chatted while sipping and nibbling pineapple and maraschinos cherries until the anticipated crowd showed up.

The crowd never came, but the show started nevertheless. There was me, Peter and Paul, the bartender one waitress and a slightly inebriated patron at the bar. I couldn't believe it. The greatest jazz piano player alive and we were the only fans there.

We feared that Erroll would cancel the show – but he didn't. In fact, there was no intermission. Erroll played a double set. We cheered and clapped like a crowd of a hundred.

The guy at the bar got drunker and drunker and kept calling out for Erroll to play Misty. Erroll Garner wrote the music to the song Misty. Johnny Burke of Route 66 fame wrote the words. The waitress kept checking at our table. Naturally the three of us didn't have an excess of money. We had to make those five dollar Hawaiian Coolers stretch. We kept busy ducking the waitress. That wasn't easy, we being the only paying customers in the place other than drunken Herman up at the bar. She kept looking over our way and we kept sucking the melted ice cubes from the bottom of our glasses quietly through our fancy straws. It would have been embarrassing if we weren't having so much fun.

I can still picture Erroll, his bass fiddle player and drummer sitting up on that stage. They were playing as if the house was packed. I'll never forget that night. I hope that Erroll was being paid by the hour and not by the number of drinks sold.

It was a fantastic night for the three of us ... not so great for the Frolics and the poor waitress.

Erroll seemed to be having a great time also. He never stopped grunting and groaning (one of his well known trademarks), smiling and playing. Herman, the drunk at the bar, was so sloshed he probably won't remember ... but if he wasn't having a good time, he sure fooled us.

Mister Five by Five
Duck Pins and Big Jim Sheehy

Duckpins were shorter and fatter than tenpins. But the duckpin bowling ball was the real difference. It was smaller than the tenpin type bowling ball, yet bigger than the candlepin bowling ball. It was just big enough so that most people could not get a grip onto it – it had no finger holes in it. You had to cradle it on your hand and wrist. It was somewhat of a balancing act. Anybody with a small hand had a good deal of trouble with the duckpin bowling ball. But with practice, like everything else, some folks became very skilled at the game. Some people could throw a looping curve ball or a reverse spin ball and all sorts of other tricky things.

We pin boys were diligent in trying to make sure that every pin was covering the *spot* exactly. If a pin were even slightly off center, the pyramid of duck pins would look distorted to the guy bowling. They were constantly screaming down the lane to us kids to move the four pin over to the left or the two pin to the right – like they were such good bowlers that it actually made a difference if a pin was off the mark here or there. But, boys will be boys and men will be men. But when setting up pins for the men, jumping up onto the perch in the back of the pit to dodge the flying duck pins was a matter of speed and urgency.

The women's league was not so threatening. The women often had difficulty just holding the ball. The balls came down the lane at about two miles an hour and often flopped into the gutter. The women rolled the balls so slowly that the pin boy could stand, fearlessly, in the pit behind the end of the lane. The pins never splattered or leaped into the air with the ladies. Setting up pins for the girls was slow and safe.

Being a pin boy was a great job. Of course, any job at all was considered as great to us kids. Not only did we make money, but we had a place to hangout all winter. We could also bowl for free. We would have to set up pins for each other but what the heck – a good deal nonetheless.

Setting up pins at the English Social on Arlington St. in the old neighborhood wasn't all fun and games. Things often got difficult. The Ray Dolan incident for example remains infamous in the anthology of *Lawrence – My Hometown* remembrances.

Ray, of course, was just one of us pin boys. He was famous among his peers for not taking any crap from anybody. He was not considered a tough guy but tough guys didn't scare him. If what you did affected Ray the wrong way, he told you so.

Ray and I and a few others were setting up after the festivities one evening when some of the ladies came in to bowl a couple of strings. Things were going along very leisurely. The ladies were throwing their gutter balls with, now and then, an occasional ball down the center of the lane. You could actually watch the ball hit and roll from one pin to the next. It was sooo slow – bonk bonk; bonk bonk. The pins would rock on their heels and occasionally fall and tumble to one side or the other. Yawn, yawn and light up another Lucky Strike.

With the ladies we simply stood in the pit behind the pins at the end of the lane. We didn't bother to waste any extra energy jumping up onto the elevated seat above the pit where we were distanced somewhat from the scattering and flying pins of the male dynamos.

Dolan and one of the other pin boys were passing their time leisurely conversing in their various pits on this particular lady's night, when into the bowling alley sneaked Bobby O'Sullivan. Bobby was an adult physically but yet lingered in the ten year old crackpot category, mentally. He tip-toed up to one of the bowling ball return racks, grabbed onto a bowling ball, ran down the approach and zinged the ball down Dolan's alley. The other pin boys yelled a warning to Dolan to no avail. Dolan couldn't get out of the pit in time. The ball hit the pins and the pins went flying. Dolan covered his head with his arms but he got smeared with flying deadwood.

Ray was not too happy by this turn of events. He started yelling at Bobby O'Sullivan from his position in the pit. Bobby screamed back calling Ray a little sissy.

The battle of words went back and forth. The women bowlers voiced their disapproval taking up cause with Dolan and chastising Bobby, the supposed adult. Bobby told one of the women where to go and shoved another off with one hand. He was a little drunk as always. Ray picked up a duckpin in each hand and started up the alley towards Bobby. Bobby laughed and egged Ray on with taunts and jibes. Finally Dolan and Bobby were nose to nose or should I say, nose to chest. Bobby grabbed Dolan by the shirt and tossed him to the floor. We all figured that Dolan was about to get his butt whipped when bounding through the swinging doors came Big Jim Sheehy.

Big Jim was the dad of one of the pin boy rank and file.

Big Jim was only about five-foot-two, but he weighed enough to be six-foot-nine. He was an original *Mister Five by Five*. He came barreling through those doors like a locomotive. He didn't hesitate for a second. He didn't say one word or shout one syllable. He was simply steaming on down the line. He barreled into Bobby O'Sullivan like a grizzly bear. When he hit Bobby he was traveling at about the speed of light – or the speed of very, very heavy. He absorbed Bobby and carried him off into the nearest wall. SLAM! Bobby was nose-slammed into the wall. We all groaned. We thought that Bobby must be dead. But his arms began to move as he tried to get a base to push himself off the wall and backwards against Mr. Sheehy. But Big Jim would have none of it. He shuffled his feet back and leaned his whole weight against Bobby. Each time that Bobby tried to move, Big Jim humped his huge belly into Bobby's backside and slammed him further into the wall.

"Apologize to the ladies and that little boy, you horses' ass."

"Like hell I will."

Slam! Slam! Slam! Big Jim's belly went bounding and pounding.

"Humph, humph, humph," gasped Bobby as the air was evacuated from his body.

I had seen a few fist fights and brawls between adult males before but none ever like this. Here we had a man beating up another man with his belly.

"Apologize you horses' ass, apologize!"

Bobby resisted and resisted and Big Jim belly-butted and butted.

Finally Bobby could take no more. None of us could believe it, big, bad Bobby at last squeaked out that he was sorry.

"Say it louder so that all the ladies and little children can hear you."

"I apologize," Bobby whimpered.

"Louder, you sorry excuse for a man! LOUDER!"

"I apologize. I APOLOGISE for God's sake."

Oomph! Big Jim gave his victim one more belly slam and then pulled away. Bobby seemed to be fastened to the wall. Then he slowly sunk down onto the floor. Big Jim turned around. He apologized to the ladies for the disturbance and waddled in his penguin-like fashion back through the swinging doors and out into the barroom where he climbed awkwardly back onto his favorite barstool.

It was all in a day's work for Big Jim, I guess. But it was mighty impressive to us kids. Big Jim was a peculiar looking specimen, but not one to be laughed at or not taken seriously. He was a man of honor. He was fearless. He rescued ladies in distress and young pin boys in over their heads. We kids were very impressed. He was always Mister Sheehy to us. Yes sir, call me Mister! Mister Sheehy, our five by five hero; a knight in the shape of a beer barrel with bright red suspenders and a wiffle haircut. He was our man of the hour – Big Bad Jim. Big Jim Sheehy, *Mister Five by Five* – a true Lawrence style American hero.

Basketball Be My Life

From the age of seven until I got to my freshman year at Central Catholic, *basketball be my life*. I carried a basketball to St. Rita's with me most days. I left my basketball in the corridor directly below my winter coat, snuggled in place between my *rubbers* or pullover, buckle-up, rubber boots.

In the winter, I often went to school carrying a basketball and a shovel. I would shovel off the court (half court) in the St. Rita's schoolyard after classes – and I wouldn't be alone. Often there were three or four of us with shovels.

We played before the snow came, after the snow arrived and even during a snow storm. We played morning, noon and night – under the streetlights. I was often late to school in the mornings, becoming overly involved in some fancy behind-the-back or between-the-legs dribbling techniques. I dribbled and practiced my lay-ups at imaginary baskets attached to telephone poles up and down Arlington St., to and from school. I bounced my professional model Voit basketball off chainlink fenses, brick walls, mail boxes and whatever, in improving my passing and shooting abilities.

I considered the Voit model basketball to be the best. It had the correct sound. It had that clunking, hard leather sound when you bounced it – not that spongy, rubber *boing* sound like many of the others. If somebody bought me anything other than a Voit basketball at Christmas time, I brought it back to the store and demanded a trade in. Voit had the best outdoor, schoolyard ball out there – and all us kids knew it.

My all-star basketball career began in the fifth grade. I think it was Father Macuska or Father Lemond who came into our fifth grade class and announced the beginnings of a new St. Rita's team that would be called the Pintos. St. Rita's already had a team called the Ponies and another called the Mustangs. The Mustangs was for the eighth graders and the Ponies was for the seventh graders. The new Pintos would be for us little guys in the fifth and sixth grade.

Father Macuska called me and Johnny Welch up to the front of the class. As we faced the class he told everybody of our precocious schoolyard careers. Me and Johnny actually felt that Father Macuska was starting this whole new division because of me and him. Of course, it was an inter-school thing involving hundreds and hundreds of little kids. But if you listened to Father Macuska, it all came about because he had heard about me and Johnny Welch and what great little basketball players we were. It was very flattering and we felt his praise of our abilities was more than overdue. We were pretty great. We were small, that's all. Besides, St. Rita was the patron of lost causes you know. So there you go.

The highlight of my grammar school basketball career came in the eighth grade. We won it all. Actually our biggest competition that year was the Ponies from St. Rita's. Big George Goodale, who was about 6'6" in the eighth grade decided not to play for the Mustangs. As a consequence St. Rita's had two championship teams that year. George is obviously still growing. He gets taller and taller every time I write about him.

The Mustangs was one of the few teams in the league who had figured out a method to beat big George. We had the Boston Celtic strategy – we beat the hell out of poor George. We got him rattled and unfortunately for George, he rattled easily.

We also had Dicky Bolton. Dicky was no taller than any of the rest of our team but he had the unique ability to jump about five feet straight up from a standing position. He would win the tap-off every time. We beat the Ponies in a playoff for the championship and had an undefeated season.

As a consequence we were awarded the privilege of playing a full court exhibition game before the *big guys* played one Friday night at Central Catholic Auditorium.

The place was packed, as it always was. The bleachers were jammed and the upstairs was standing room only. This was really big for a bunch of Lawrence eighth graders. We were all nervous and very excited. On our Mustang team there was me and some other guys.

Isn't that terrible? How self-involved can one person get? I know Dicky Bolton was on that team and Johnny Welch and maybe John Medvekey ... maybe John Brain too. I have since been told that I have this story all wrong and that George Goodale was with us that year. I don't remember it that way.

Since we had defeated all the eighth grade school teams in our division, they felt that they had to get us some stiffer competition. We would be forced to play the future professional criminals from the Essex County Training School.

Essex Training may have had a few cows and a pig here and there but rumor had it that the kids there kept killing them and eating them ... raw.

Essex Training School was considered to be a reform school. I met a guy recently who got sent there as a child and at seventy-three years of age he was still recanting his harrowing days at good old Essex Training School. He sounded much the same to me as a Holocaust victim – except he was Catholic and not Jewish. He felt that the only really, really mean, criminal type people there, were the guardians who ran the joint.

He was not happy about his experience and claimed innocence. We kids from the streets of Lawrence felt, "There for the grace of God go I." Our attitude was that those kids got caught and we didn't.

It was interesting though, as the Essex Training School guys came bounding out of the locker room, they were frisked by the authorities. They weren't into body searches in those days though.

They found a couple of screwdrivers, a few Skillsaw blades and some very pointy nails but nothing serious. Two or three of the guys looked to be more my father's age. There was one guy who must have been the stand-in for the plow-pulling ox out on the farm. He was gigantic – and covered with muscles. I think he grew up to become Killer Kowalski of champion wresting fame.

All us little guys on the Mustangs watched these guys being frisked at the locker room door and we wondered as we stood out there at center court why the Marist Brothers at Central Catholic who were in charge of this thing had decided that we should be murdered in front of all these people. What was this, something from the old Roman Coliseum days, or what?

Let the games begin. And the emperor says ... thumbs down. Gee whiz, we would have gladly played St Patrick's once again. They didn't have a kid over three feet tall. Maybe we could have spotted them a few points. What? That's fair.

The St. Rita's Mustangs against Murder Incorporated? What was this all about? Were they also going to sacrifice a couple of virgins before this all took off?

As it turned out these guys from the Training School were big and brawny but very sloppy and uncoordinated. They played a schoolyard type of ball that we were all very accustomed to – lots of wild elbows, pushing and shoving under the boards and bunches of low blows and shots to the kidneys when the ref wasn't looking.

I went diving for a ball behind Killer Kowalski and he nearly knocked my two front teeth out with a sharp and meaty elbow to the chops. They actually stopped the game and the referee came over and tried to wiggle my two front teeth. "No, they're still in there pretty good," he said, "Play ball!" The crowd cheered wildly ... for me!

Pretty good? I thought that was a little worrisome.

We won the game and got a big trophy for St. Rita's. It was an exciting night. I made a couple of big baskets that even surprised me. I remember dribbling down the right side of the court and into the corner for my prized double handed, over the shoulder heave-ho shot. I had temporarily forgotten that we were playing full court. When I looked up before throwing the ball, the basket appeared to be in another county. I said holy cow and put an extra heave-ho into the regular heave-ho and the darn thing went off the backboard and in. The crowd came to their feet and the place went bonkers.

I did a fake to my right and then turn to the left hook shot from the foul line and got another rousing cheer from the crowd.

I guess the excitement from that night filled me up for basketball. I never played much after that. I didn't play in high school. I don't even remember playing pick-up games in the schoolyard. I must have figured that was good enough for me.

Unfortunately I was never much of a stick-with-it kind of a guy. I've managed to find a reason to quit just about everything that I have ever tried – for one reason or another.

There are only three things that I've managed to stick with all these years.

I have always liked music and I took up the drums as a teenager. I play to jazz records. I never got very professional but I still have a trap set out in the shed and I still go out there and get lost in my own thoughts and imagination. I have only played with another actual human being once in my life. It was at Jimmy Rowan's wedding. I was, once again, one of the drunk ushers.

I took up writing as a freshman at Northern Essex Community College and found myself addicted. I tried to kick the habit several times throughout the course of my life, but I just haven't been able to do it. I think it is my religion – without it, this life makes no sense to me. I've even tried quitting based on the grounds that quitting is the thing I do best in life. But even that didn't work. If I'm not writing something, I feel … empty and lost. All philosophers, I have read, write their ideas in an attempt to justify their lives. I think that the fact that I am here is enough justification. My writing is inspired by Kilroy. You remember … Kilroy was here. Well, Richard was here too.

The third is my wife, Carol. I don't know if it is that I just won't quit her or that for reasons beyond my limited understanding, she just won't quit me. But whatever, here we are, *still travelin' on and singin' our song … side by side. In all kinds of weather … whether it's rain or snow … here we are together…* or something like that. I'm not good at memorizing words to songs either. I get lost rather easy too. But when it happens, I don't sit down and cry anymore. I'm a grown-up now.

Strip Joints

Lawrence has always been the cultural and intellectual capital of greater New England as all of us past graduates realize but unfortunately – or fortunately, depending on your point of view – Lawrence did have an underclass and a seamy side. Strip joints were a part of this less than proper side of Lawrence.

Strip joints 100 years from today will be looked upon as the aberrations of a sexual repressed, immature culture, I'm sure. But I must note that as women have come of age in this sexually repressed, deplorable male culture of ours, they chose to exercise their new freedom by popularizing male strip joints and other male perversions as opposed to eradiating the practices that they so traditionally loathed when the shoe was on the other foot – or was off the other foot, as the case may be.

I have also been surprised by women's active participation in the brutal, traditionally male sport of war. Instead of championing the abolition of the practice, women have chosen to join the Marines and place doilies in our tanks and paint cute lipstick designs on our bazookas. Their behavior makes the devilish, cynic in me smile confidently.

I remember only two such strip joints. The English Social Club on the corner of Hampshire and Center St. stands out first in my memory. As pin boys at the English

Social Club our gang had a special access to this unique art form.

The Chez-When on the corner of Hampshire and Methuen St. was the other that I remember.

In comparing these two cultural centers, I would have to put the English Social Club in the B class and the Chez-When in the A class.

I remember standing at the crowded bar at the English Social Club and occasionally looking over my shoulder at one of these exotic dancers. Most of them were my mother's age and many had a similar shape – rather babushka-like. I often thought to myself that these poor, older women must have really needed the money. But I know they thought of themselves as professionals.

I remember one lady twirling one of her tassels off and running from the exhibition floor in total embarrassment. After she gathered her tassel from the floor, she dashed by the bar. She looked at me and my buddies with total fear in her eyes and exclaimed, "I've never been so embarrassed in my life!" She was embarrassed because she had spun off one of her nipple covers or tassels? I was somewhat confused but sympathetic nonetheless.

Most of these women did not garner a great amount of attention. The men and women who went to the English Social Club would have been there whether there were strippers appearing or not. The English Social Club was the social spot of the neighborhood for a period. The crowd would be so uninvolved with the exotic dancers that the dancers would become annoyed. One professional dancer became so upset that she put her thumb and forefinger into her mouth and let go a blearing whistle. The mulling crowd stopped and everyone turned to the dance floor. The chubby exotic dancer placed her hands onto her hips and said, "Okay, what does a girl have to do to get some attention around here?" There was a moment of silence while everyone put her question before their mental processes. Finally someone shouted, "Why don't you try standing on your head."

The dancer thought for a moment and then cued the band. The bass player nudged the old man playing the piano and once aroused from his nap the salacious music began to bump and grind in full burlesque fashion. Immediately, Suzie from Saskatchewan fell to her knees, lowered her head to the floor and began the attempt to stand on her head. Within moments the audience was at full attention. A crowd gathered around the dance floor and people in the back rows climbed up onto their chairs. The applause and screams were deafening. I don't remember her succeeding in her attempt to stand on her head but she definitely succeeded in getting the attention of the crowd.

The Chez-When, on the other hand, was much more sophisticated. They actually had young, attractive strippers. The drinking crowd was younger also. I remember catching a glimpse of one of my older, established Chelmsford St. neighbors bellying up to the bar one evening. I was totally shocked to see a man of his reputation in such an establishment. Strangely enough I thought nothing unusual of a man of my stature being there dribbling at the mouth next to him. And so it goes.

The management at the Chez actually hired a cop to be on hand to make sure things did not get out of control.

The entertainers often appeared in character. One emulated Marylyn Monroe, another Mae West and others a variety of unique Hollywood greats.

Some were into dancing techniques and others were into props and unique, visual aides. Some of these dancers, with their various props – beer bottles, broomstick, eye glasses, jump ropes etc. – did things that I have never seen repeated anywhere. Of course, I don't know why anyone would want to repeat such contortions, but, nevertheless, this fact remains true to this very day.

The policeman who was there every week was there to keep the dancers in check in addition to holding the crowd in their seats. Massachusetts, proper and puritanical, did not allow total nudity in any performance. So the cop was there to be sure that neither the exotic dancer nor any of the audience became totally nude, I presume. There was this neighborhood girl who had this thing with her socks ... but I won't get into that today.

There was never any total nudity at the Chez until the on duty cop went outside to smoke his cigarette. Why the cop went outside in the middle of every act to smoke a cigarette, I don't know. The smoke was so thick inside the Chez one could cut it with a butcher's knife. Maybe he wanted to smoke where the air was cleaner. But once he was gone, then the tassels would fly and the infamous crotch shots would begin. It was a strange time, very strange indeed.

Of course, you may be asking yourselves how I have such intimate details of these type establishments. Well, I am a reporter you will remember! I have also conducted numerous interviews with people who frequented these type sleazy places. In addition, I have many secret sources. The nature of this material being what it is, I can not release any of these sources – unless they start ratting on me. In that case, I will send you all their names and addresses and possibly a nude photo ... of them, not me.

Alma Meter

We have all heard a million times the old cliché that children can be cruel. Of course, it should go without saying that adults can be even crueler. There are comedy artists today who make their living being crude, rude, obnoxious and cruel. Where have all the Red Skeltons, Jimmy Durantes and Jack Bennys gone? But I hesitate to go in that direction, like Bob Cousy and Easy Ed McCauley, or Charlie "Choo Choo" Justice, dropping these names will get me nowhere. Grown men will look at me in bewilderment and teenagers will shrug their shoulders and giggle. There are teens today who don't even know who George Washington was, never mind Bob Cousy.

Alma Meter was the name my buddy Ray Dolan christened the poor old woman who lived across the street from Nell's Variety Store on the corner of Center St. and Exchange.

Now before I tell this horror story let me put in a disclaimer. We little punks hanging out all over the street corners of Lawrence back in my day were all good Christians. We were even better than good Christians – we were Roman Catholics. We all went to church every Sunday. We went to Confession and Communion regularly. Most of us were taught by nuns and in our homes one could find a crucifix on nearly every wall. There were businesses in Lawrence that sold nothing but holy stuff.

There was a little store up by St. Mary Church where you could buy bibles, rosary beads, laminated holy pictures and even small plastic containers containing a sliver of bone from one of the twelve Apostles or St. Francis of Assisi.

I never understood how the bones of St. Francis could still be selling centuries later. But, I suppose, under the penumbra of St. Francis could have came anyone or anything that St. Francis ever came in contact with – that also had bones. Then, of course, one should not discount or underestimate miracles. Miracle kits were not for sale at that time in Lawrence by Roman Catholic Holy Stores. I think Oral Roberts reincarnated that bit of holy mercantilism. But he was a Protestant and what can you expect from those type people anyway?

We were all good, Roman Catholic boys. We took off our hats when we passed by a church and blessed ourselves when passing where the altar would be inside the church. Some guys would even genuflect. We would often kiss the gold crosses hanging around our necks after cursing or saying something harsh. We blessed ourselves to ward off any type of danger and to show respect – before fist fights, borrowing other people's automobiles, hoping trains, or even going into a corner store to steal penny candy – anything that took extra-ordinary courage. Good Roman Catholic girls often blessed themselves before having pre-marital sex under the pier at the Five O'clock Club at Salisbury Beach. I can testify to the truth of that example myself. I realize that it was shameful and embarrassing ... but I got over it.

But poor Alma, bless her heart, she tried to do everything to get rid of us, the many angelic, moronic mistakes of the accepted Rhythm Method. Yes, our parents did have Rhythm and lots of it.

Alma would come out of her little cottage nearly every afternoon to voice her democratic right to life, liberty and the pursuit of her happiness. The problem was that everybody in the neighborhood felt that they had a right to happiness too. And their happiness did not include any of us wandering angels who were the living, breathing results of our parents own personal pursuit of their individual happiness and joy.

We had our footballs and basketballs stabbed by the pocket knives of unappreciative tenement dwellers. We were threatened, badgered and harassed from one corner to another. Unfortunately for Alma, the Nell's Corner directly across from her little cottage in *Paradise Lost* was where we decided to make our stand. The adults of the surrounding area would have to make a decision as to what to do with us. We would stand our ground. Put us in prison, send us to boot camp, send us to a reservation, threaten, cajole, harass and browbeat – we weren't moving. It was the Last Stand of the Howard Ass.

"Do you boys have mothers and fathers?" Alma would ask.

"No," we would tell her. "All our parents were killed in the war. But we are available for adoption. You don't have to adopt all of us. You could just take Dolan for example. After you got used to him then maybe you could take a few more of us."

"Go away!" she would scream in her broken English. "Go home where you belong or I'm going inside to call the police."

"Lady, we don't belong anywhere. You are missing the whole point. We are all mistakes that are beyond correction. You are not getting it lady."

"Ask for Officer Marynowitz. I like him the best. He got some funny jokes."

"No ask for Foley. I know his brother."

The next afternoon she would be back leaning on her fence interrupting our game of *outs* once again.

Outs were played by two kids – one hitting and one fielding. We would pitch a High Bouncer or a soft sponge rubber ball at varying speeds against the curbing or the tenement steps. A single was a ground ball the fielder didn't catch; a double was a ball that passed the fielder in the air; a triple was a fly ball off Alma Meter's house; and a home run was a high fly that landed on top of Alma Meter's roof. It was a pitched roof, so don't worry, our ball always rolled back down to us.

"You boys are all going to hell, you know."

"We are? I thought we were already there. Did you hear that? This ain't hell."

"Well, I'll be darned; we still have something to look forward to. Alma, what is hell like? Do you know? You ever been there?"

"Yes, I have been there and I know you boys will find out. It is filled with fire and you will burn forever."

"Come on Alma, you're exaggerating – not forever? Forever is way too long. Maybe we will burn for a month or a year?"

"Oh no … oh no, you boys will burn forever and forever."

"Alma, you know, most of us guys really like you. Why are you so mean?"

"I'M MEAN? YOU THINK THAT I AM MEAN?"

"Who here thinks that Alma Meter is mean?" Everybody raised their hand. Alma Meter shuffled back into her cottage shaking her head in disbelief.

A week or so later Alma played her biggest hole card. She came slowly around the corner of her cottage carrying something wrapped in a towel. She stood at her fence staring at us venomously. We all knew she was up to something serious. We stopped banging our rubber ball off the curb and gave Alma our undivided attention. She smiled witch-like. Then she revealed what she had been concealing under her towel. She quickly ripped away the towel and flashed us with a picture. It was a picture of Jesus Christ displaying his Sacred Heart.

"Do you boys know this man?" she asked with a small smirk.

We all left our positions and walked over to her fence. We examined her picture closely. Finally one of us said, "No, I have never seen that guy before in my life. Any of you guys know who that is?" Everybody looked at the picture more closely and then we all shook our heads negatively and mumbled to one another the mystery of the identity behind her picture. "Who is it Alma, one of your kids?"

"This is GOD!" Alma screamed.

"Oh come on. No one can take a picture of God. That's Mr. Alma Meter dressed up like God. You can't fool us Alma. Come on, come clean. It's your husband ain't it?"

Alma quickly blessed herself six or seven times. She coved the picture again with her towel.

"You boys will all be going to hell. If there is one thing that I am positive about, God will not allow any of you devils into heaven." She continued blessing herself the entire distance back to her front door. Before entering her cottage she shook her fist at us and prophesized our dismal future one last time.

Believe it or not we did feel sorry for old Alma Meter. We took our game of outs around the corner and bounced our ball off two other houses. We stopped playing outs off Alma's house entirely. We determined that she was taking this situation much, much too seriously. How could God send a bunch of cute kids like us to hell? It was ridiculous.

Interestingly enough I never confessed harassing poor Alma Meter to a priest. Obviously I never felt our behavior to be a serious sinful transgression. I doubt if any of my buddies did either. So let me say on behalf of all of us – Bless me Father for I have sinned. It has been a very long time since my last confession. Father, I was a voluntary participant in driving poor Alma Meter nearly out of her poor, immigrant mind. My only excuse is that we were cruel little children created in your image and likeness preparing to join the world and become cruel, obnoxious grown ups with an image and likeness all our own. Forgive us Father for it does seem that none of us knew what he was doing. Amen.

English with Brother Stanislaus

"Good morning class."
"Good morning Brother Stanislaus."
"Hey Bruddah?"
"Yes Mr. Jeworsky?"
"How come you ain't got nothin' written on the blackboard dis mornin'?"
"Ahhh? Very good, Jeworsky. It is interesting that you should ask that question and even more interesting that you phrased it as you have. Pay attention, Jeworsky."
Brother Stanislaus turned and wrote on the Blackboard.
"Jeworsky, what have I written on the blackboard?"
Jeworsky reads aloud, "What is the rule for the double negative?"
"Very good, and … what is the rule for the double negative, Mr. Jeworsky?"
"Ahh … I ain't got no idea, Bruddah."
"You haven't? Why does that not surprise me?"
"I don't know, maybe you ain't got no idea eedah, Bruddah."
"Oh but I do, I do … Anyone else?"
Silence.
"Come on now? Anyone can answer. Does anyone know the rule for the double negative?"
More quiet, followed by additional silence. Brother Stanislaus looks around the class seeking someone else to

embarrass. Boys begin ducking behind the torso of the boy sitting in front of them. Others sink down into their seats in an attempt to get their heads below the level of their desks.

Brother Stanislaus smiles and returns to the blackboard and writes. "Mr. Jeworsky, please read what I have just written on the blackboard."

Jeworsky reads, "The rule for the double negative is ... Do not use the double negative."

"Very good. Now Mr. Jeworsky, can you give me an example of a double negative in a sentence?"

"I ain't got no idea, Bruddah."

"Very good Jeworsky. You see class, Mr. Jeworsky has just given us a perfect example of a double negative. Mr. Jeworsky said, *'He ain't got no idea.'* Actually ain't isn't even a word but ..."

"It ain't?"

"No it isn't."

"Why ain't it?"

"It just isn't. In fact, if you look in a dictionary you will not find ain't in it."

"You have got to be kidding me? Ain't ain't in the dictionary?"

"No it ain't ... I mean, no it isn't"

"Well Bruddah, maybe you better get a bigger dictionary because everybody I know uses the word ain't." The class all nods their heads in agreement with Jeworsky.

"It may be used colloquially by you and your friends and even in the neighborhood but technically ain't isn't a word."

"Well, I'll tell ya Bruddah, *colocoly* might not be a word but ain't is a word and everybody uses it. If everybody knows it and everybody uses it, it must be a word. How can a word that everybody uses everyday, not be a word?"

"Okay, let's skip it for now and get back to, *I ain't got no idea.* We'll just forget about ain't not being a word and push forward. When you say, *I ain't got no idea,* you have used a double negative. Because you have used two negatives in the same sentence you have actually said the opposite of what you intended to say. You were trying to express the notion that you were without an idea. But because you employed a double negative you actually said that you had an idea. You see, you said, *I ain't got no idea.* This is stating that you don't have *no idea*, which is really saying that you have an idea. If you don't have no ideas then you must have some ideas. You see, if you don't have NO idea, then you must have an idea or some ideas. You get me?"

"No Bruddah, I said exactly what I meant to say. I ain't got no idea. That means I ain't got no idea. And I don't got NO idea, believe me."

"Yes ... well, everybody take out a pencil and a piece of paper. We are going to have a pop quiz."

Everybody starts rustling around in the open compartments under their seats looking for paper and pencil.

"I ain't got no pencil, Bruddah."

"You ain't got no pencil, Jeworsky?"

"No Bruddah, I ain't got none."

Brother Stanislaus rubs his chin and ponders. "Okay, who else ain't got no pencil?"

"I ain't got one nieddah, Bruddah."

"You ain't got one nieddah? Very good. Anyone who ain't got no pencil come forward because I have some extra pencils in my drawer and I will provide you with one."

"Hey Bruddah, that's great but what if I ain't got no paper eedah?"

"You ain't got no pencil and you ain't got no paper? Jeworsky, why do you bother coming to school?"

"It's where the bus stops, Bruddah."

"No Jeworsky not THIS school, any school?"

"My parents don't want me to go to any school, Bruddah. They want me to come here to Central Catholic sos that I can get a good education, learn somethin' important and become somethin' when I grow up."

"What is it that you would like to become when you finish your education here at Central Catholic and you grow up, Mr. Jeworsky?"

"Anything, Bruddah."

"Well, you know Jeworsky, I think you will be successful. I think that one day if you proceed as you have been, you will definitely be able to be anything … if not anything, certainly you can become something."

"Thank-you, Bruddah. I appreciate that."

"You are very welcome, Jeworsky."

The bell rings ending the class.

"Okay, hold up! I want those pencils back. FELLAS, the pencils? Well, okay," Brother Stanislaus shouts, "bring the pencils back with you tomorrow. We will be having a quiz. Don't forget. You don't got no pencil tomorrow and you are in big trouble. You all heard me now."

Everybody is pushing and shoving racing out the back door. There is too much commotion and chatter. Nobody can hear anything. It is inevitable. They ain't got no pencils today and tomorrow they won't have none neiddah.

The Infamous Pothole

The schoolyard basketball court at St. Rita's was really nothing to brag about but nevertheless it saw a lot of action. For a number of my early years, I lived there.

The backboards were metal and half-mooned shaped as I remember. Very rarely did either of the rims have a net. On the very rare occasions when Mr. Fitzgibbons, the janitor/handyman hung a net on one of the baskets, it never lasted more than a week. We were hard on nets for some reason. I don't understand it because most of us could not jump and touch the bottom of the net. We would have contests where we ran and leaped. At my best and my tallest I was only able to nick it at the bottom. Some of the bigger guys from King Tut's could grab onto it. Sometimes a quarter of a net would hang on, dangling by a hook or two on the rim and we would use it as a guide for months.

We didn't have anybody dunking the ball in those days. I can remember the first time I ever saw a player dunk the ball. It was at the Central Catholic auditorium. My older brother Ernie and the varsity team were scrimmaging the Merrimack College Freshman team in an exhibition game. The center for Merrimack College brought the gymnasium crowd to its feet when in the warm up he leaped and stuffed the ball in the basket. He went on to perform the spectacular feat several more times. I felt sorry for my brother who would have to guard such a phenomenon. We had high hopes but the varsity lost.

Over time a hole broke loose in the asphalt at the uphill end of the St. Rita's schoolyard court. The court was asphalt and stone as I remember and it had a good downhill slant to it. We rarely used the full court or the downhill end of the court. We concentrated our energies to the uphill end but, unfortunately, that darn hole kept growing and growing.

It was on the right side of the basket, facing the basket. It started as a tiny sinkhole of sorts but it grew steadily. We adapted to it. Most of us regulars knew instinctively when to jump and where to land. We developed shots around the hole – pull-up before the hole jump shots, stop at the edge of the hole and fade away, spin away from the hole and faint, and long, leaping double pump lay-ups over the hole. We would often lead our opponents into a twisted ankle by driving just the right distance from the hole and having them step into it.

Though strategically viable, it was still a pain in the butt for all of us. We petitioned Bill the janitor countless times but he never could seem to get to it. Finally Bobby Pappalardo twisted his ankle for the last time. "I'm never playing here again," he screamed sitting on the pavement and rubbing his ankle. We all comforted him as he limped and moaned all the way to his house. He lived just around the corner from St. Rita's – kitty-corner from Jimmy Costello's and just past Jessie's penny candy and school supply store on Arlington St.

We all agreed that Bobby was right. That hole was something else. We had tried everything. We had filled it over and over with dirt and pebbles but nothing worked. It always washed away or disappeared. As we sat on Bobby's front step discussing the situation, Dickey Michaud whose dad was a house painter and handyman suggested that we build our own portable basket.

Kids instantly know a good idea when they hear one and we were all off and running. With a portable basket we could make our own basketball court wherever we wanted.

Michaud scrounged up some plywood, 2 x 4s and the necessary tools. Bobby had an old rim in his back yard. We nailed the backboard to a couple of 2 x 4s and then screwed the rim through the backboard and the 2 x 4s and attached the other end of the 2 x 4s to a rectangular platform base – being absolutely sure that the rim would be exactly 10 feet from the ground. But it was still a little wobbly. We added some plywood to the front and both sides of our platform base. It appeared to be perfect until we tried to stand it up. It was top heavy and kept tumbling forward. We could stabilize it by having one kid stand on the back of the platform. But that turned out to be very dangerous and annoying. We found a bucket and filled it with rocks and set it onto the back of our platform. It worked like a charm.

Though the engineering was perfect it still had a flaw here and there. Flaw number one was its portability. It was a four kid minimum portable basket – not counting the kid necessary for the bucket of rocks. But that was no problem in our neighborhood we always had more kids than necessary for any task.

We decided that the best place to put our portable basket was in the middle of Arlington St. between Bobby Pappalardo's house and Russ Brown's house across the street. Though the pavement on Arlington St. was good and smooth the traffic presented a problem. There weren't all that many cars going up and down Arlington St. in those days but enough to be aggravating.

For some reason people who owned automobiles were under the impression that paved roads were made exclusively for them and their autos. We, of course, felt otherwise and we debated accordingly. We argued that there were kids long before there were automobiles. We were able to get some older and weaker drivers to back up and turn onto Willow St. but the younger, tougher guys made us move our portable basket and let them through.

We then tried our portable basket on the corner of Exchange St. next to Jimmy Costello house. But that was worse. Cars coming down Exchange St. would have to back all the way to Center St. They wouldn't do it.

We finally decided to use the Arlington and Exchange St. corner of the St. Rita's schoolyard. The original court was on the Hampshire St. side of the school. Unfortunately the darn gate was locked with a big chain after school hours so we had to hump it over the six foot chainlink fence. That would be difficult but worth the effort we all felt.

The Arlington/Exchange St. side was perfect – no holes. There was a little problem with the school windows though.

We could set our portable basket up with its back to the street but then a missed shot often went over the fence and out onto the street. We opted to use the school building (windows and all) as our backstop.

We did well for a time. Mr. Fitzgibbons, it seemed, enjoyed replacing glass windows more than he did patching holes in the pavement. He confronted us one Saturday afternoon as we were humping our portable basket over the Exchange St. fence and enquired as to our objective. We told him about our twisted ankles and that damn hole. He didn't get all grouchy and bent out of shape. He complimented us on our ingenuity. He even helped us get our portable basket over the fence. But later that evening he returned. He asked us all to come over to the Hampshire St. side of the schoolyard.

Upon inspection we found our hole filled with new asphalt and all padded down hard and firm. We returned to the Hampshire St. side of the St. Rita's schoolyard to play basketball.

But today every time I see one of those portable plastic basketball setups, I think of our four-kid, semi-portable basket and think that we were almost millionaires. We had a portable basketball hoop before anybody else ever wanted one. Talk about being ahead of your time! We were right there ... almost.

Canobie Lake Park

First thing one should know about Canobie Lake is that like Gloucester and Worchester its spelling has nothing to do with its pronunciation. Gloucester is Glah-stah and Worchester is, of course, Wuss-stah and Canobie Lake is actually one word – Canabalake – Canabal rhyming with Hannibal and lake becoming *ake*. So you end up with Canabal–ake. But it is really not separated into two syllables. It is not Canabal-ake; it is Canabalake. You must say it fast and all in one breathe ... Canabalake.

My biggest memory of Canabalake is not the lake or the park but the Wasmaco ice cream stand just down the road from the entrance to the park. On many a warm Sunday afternoon my Uncle Ray would take us all for a ride out to Wasmaco's to get a cone. Going for a ride in a car was once considered a treat. It was a recreational experience.

One dip was a nickel and two dips a dime. And don't tell me that all prices are irrelevant or proportional. I was living on nothing a month in 1964 and I am living on nothing a month in 2010.

We could not get back into my uncle's car until we completely finished our cones. My Uncle Ray's cars were bought new and they stayed new until trade-in time.

On my very first trip, I remember wanting three dips. My uncle suggested that I get one and if I finished that maybe next time he might allow me two. One dip was enormous and two dips were gigantic. But I do remember getting two dips because I would get two different flavors sometimes.

I was heavy on black cherry for a time; then orange pineapple had me for awhile. Then there was always chocolate and the New England favorite, coffee. Rocky Road with the marshmallows was always good, as was peach, strawberry and blueberry – chunks of real peaches and whole blueberries and strawberries. For the longest time I developed a serious addiction to something called Frozen Pudding. It was touted as containing a portion of rum – some places called it Rum Raisin – but Frozen Pudding was big around the neighborhood. Even Clifford's Ice Cream Parlor on the corner of Chelmsford and Lawrence Streets sold Frozen Pudding.

Clifford had a deal on half gallons. You could get a half gallon for 99 cents. I never understood Clifford on that one. All of his prices except for those hand-packed, half gallons were very futuristic. All us kids figured that Mr. Clifford was ahead of his time when it came to pricing and portions. You can get a hot dog on the interstate today for the same price Mr. Clifford charged back in 1952. We all felt that Mr. Clifford was into playing his prized Gulbranson organ much, much more than waiting on customers. I think deep down inside he found customer's annoying – and having been in the ice cream business myself, I agree. For ten years I seriously pondered the philosophical question – Why children? I think that every high school should have a mandatory course entitled – "Why children? Are they really necessary?"

My Uncle Ray was also instrumental in getting me and a friend our first real job. We were hired to put up Christmas decorations in the roller skating rink at *Canabalake*. This experience remains in my mind like a chamber of horrors. We had to string green garland and holly on metal cables that ran just under the 9000 foot high ceiling. The manager, Simon LaSadist, had two ladders, previously used in the construction of the Empire State Building in New York, positioned for the Great Climb.

Halfway up the ladder I was screaming inside. I checked over at my buddy on the other ladder. He was hugging the rungs like they were his Teddy Bear. My chuckling uncle and his ex-German prisoner of war camp Commandedstaffenflugel looked like specks down on the skating floor below. I can still see my little buddy's huge, glazed, brown adrenalin-induced, naturally dilated eyes as he stared out into no place in particular. His face screamed out, "Oh God please help me!"

Prior to this experience, I was under the impression that my Uncle Ray loved me. I questioned that assumption. Maybe it was not quite love. Maybe it was obligation of some sort. Maybe he had problems growing up himself and really never found childhood that appealing. Maybe he didn't find MY childhood all that appealing. I also wondered why these two grown men would not accept this hazardous duty themselves. Certainly my little buddy and me had more possible future than either of them two adult clowns put together. There they were, way down there on the hard, safe floor. What were we guinea pigs or what?

When we dropped my speechless friend off at his house, he leaped out of the car and ran for his life. I don't remember him playing with me ever again. My uncle was still laughing. In the future whenever my uncle said that he knew of someone who was looking for help, I immediately informed my uncle that I was already committed to another duty. He would smile.

I think I took my first roller coaster ride at *Canabalake*. The teenage girl in the car in front of me kept screaming at me to be a *big boy* and open my eyes. I remember thinking I would like to tell her that I would show her *big boy* after this ride was over if she was interested. I mean after all I was only seventeen or eighteen years of age at that time. I was still a baby for god's sake. Riding the roller coaster with my eyes closed was a long way from sitting on the green bench on the Dobby Horses. I think I was fourteen before I got on an actual Dobby Horse – and it was one that didn't go up and down. I had no aspirations of ever becoming a stunt man in the movies. I felt that I was very courageous in standing tall against people who constantly called me a chicken. Of course I was a chicken. Any normal sensible child when facing such social insanity as up and down wooden Dobby Horses and roller coasters should by natural instinct be chicken. It made sense to me.

Big Stars appeared at the ballroom at Canabalake. It was called the Canobie Lake Park's Dancehall Theater – Frank Sinatra, Tony Bennett, Ella Fitzgerald, Guy Lombardo, Duke Ellington, Sonny and Cher and Aerosmith to name a few. My Uncle Ray was a big ballroom dancer. He went to Canabalake to dance often.

Canabalake was a big deal. It was like a permanent carnival. Carnivals came and set up every year in Lawrence. The one I remember was usually in the big field that was across from the jail on Hampshire St., across from the Spicket River. We always walked through that field to get to the Immaculate Conception Church on Sunday mornings.

Canobie Lake Park was actually opened in 1902 and it hasn't missed a summer since. It is still going strong today. They have three roller coasters – the Yankee Cannonball, a 1930s type wooden roller coaster; the Canobie Corkscrew, formally the Chicago Loop and a kiddie coaster called the Dragon. Canobie Lake celebrated its 100th anniversary in 2002.

Hart's Package Store

The drug of choice for my generation Lawrencian street elf was alcohol. We started at a very early age. I remember the first sip of Muscatel I sneaked from the fridge. It was so bad. I could not understand the attraction. My fist sip of beer received an equally poor reception. But …

So there we were (the Howard version of the Bowery Boys) staked out around Hart's package store on Lawrence St. We had already sent in most of the older looking guys. They were all laughed out of the store by the owner. We were waiting for an unfamiliar face – preferably a man with a large red nose and a meandering, uncoordinated step. Finding such a man was a rather expensive proposition. As our package store representative, each *agent* claimed to be providing us with a very low commission rate or service charge – in truth they acted more like Lehman Brothers, Charles Schwab, or Liberty Mutual. They were taking the Bowery Boys for a ride.

In the past we hired such agents as we found sleeping in the coal bin at Cronin's Coal Company on Hampshire St., or May and Mary, ladies who were known to do *anything* for a drink. To these girls we were like a free ride – all profit with no bed tax. But most notorious of them all was, Billy the Bum, self-proclaimed King of the Hoboes.

Billy came wandering out of the woods one day up at the Howard Playstead. He was something right out of the

Adventures of Huck Fin or *Tom Sawyer* – like Injun Joe or some of Mark's other infamous theatricals. Billy had story after story. It was from Billy that we learned of such things as: the National Hobo Convention celebrated in Britt, Iowa since 1900; the differences between a Hobo and a Bum; riding the rails; making a Mulligan stew; Hobo script and the infamous Hobo jungles.

Billy made no advances towards the position of Liquor Store Agent for the Howard Bowery Boys, we solicited his services. He was very exacting in giving us the details of his purchases on our behalf. I guess there was no such thing as a sales slip back in those ancient times.

But Billy only showed up at certain times of the year. It was imperative that we founded our own agency. We often fell upon that big, red-nosed man with a meandering step but we yearned for the day when one of our gang could present a suitable image.

We finally found such an image in the deceptive maturity of a young man in the gang. Togo was big and burly and was shaving by the age of twelve.

Togo had this air of old about him. He was a very large child. He was swarthy complected and tough looking. We badgered Togo to accept this challenge. This could mean big savings for the gang as a whole and provide needed revenue for future gang investments (hockey sticks and chess boards). Togo agreed to step up and give it a shot.

He wore his old man overcoat, work boots and I think may have even doffed a felt hat. The night was cold and it was snowing lightly when Togo went sauntering into Hart's. We were all huddled in a lump away from the entrance to the store hanging onto someone's chainlink fence.

The tension was excruciating. It seemed like Togo was taking forever. Maybe old man Hart had finally lost it and called the cops. Togo could be inside handcuffed to the liquor counter. What should we do?

Finally Togo came strolling out with a shopping bag full of quart bottles – they could have been either Black Label or Narragansett GIQ's; those were our favorites.

"What the hell took you so long?"

"I was shooting the breeze with old Mr. Hart. I was telling him all about my kids and the work at the mill."

"Come on – you're kidding?"

"No, I told him all about the boys and little Susan, my youngest."

"Oh brother, you better remember all that hooey when you show up next week."

"No problem. I got a brain like a bank vault."

"Yeah right! Empty, heavily guarded and usually closed."

"Well, you are entitled to your opinion but I got the booze, didn't I?"

From that day forward we were independent brokers. We bought our own shares and pocketed the commission.

Togo was our liquor rep from age thirteen forward. I presume he kept his family history straight for Mr. Hart. Old Mr. Hart was still asking me for ID when I was twenty-six years old for god sake.

As time passed, there were three of us who would meet every Friday night – payday. I worked at the First National on Broadway, Togo worked at the Stop and Shop further down Broadway and Jimmy worked at the new Stop & Shop between Chelmsford and Spruce Streets.

Jimmy was the only one with a car. He would pick us up and we were off to PJ's Pizza on Broadway and then to Hart's on Lawrence St. We would get Italian meat pies and Sicilian style pizza (thicker crust – more to eat) and then head up to the baseball dugouts at the Howard. We would sit in the dugout and gorge ourselves. On those cold, snowy winter nights, we would remain in Jimmy's car with the heater on and the windows fogged up, slobbering our way through the evening discussing world affairs and laughing and joking about all the failings of our respective employers and supervisors in particular.

I'm not kidding when I say I can still taste that beer. Beer had a flavor in those by-gone days that just doesn't exist today. Maybe some of these new mini-breweries today can match that flavor, but I don't know.

The teams of surgeons and medical people who now supervise my behavior have told me that my liver has had enough beer. I question their medical expertise and I am searching for a second opinion. I'm looking for a Doctor whose last name is Narragansett – Dr. Robert Narragansett or Dr. Rupert Narragansett maybe. I don't think a Dr. Nancy Narragansett will do the trick. Women have always harbored this innate prejudice toward drunken men. I don't get it. It must be a girl thing. Of course, the meat pies and pizza were not and still aren't heart happy food choices either.

Shooting Pool
And Bowling For Dollars

I doubt that there was any boy raised in Lawrence who couldn't shoot pool or bowl.

We had duckpin, tenpin and candlepin bowling. I'm sure you all know how bowling is played but candlepin bowling might be a mystery to most of you.

In Lawrence we had the Candlepin Lanes across from the Chez-When on the corners of Amesbury and Methuen Streets. We called it *The Rec*.

It was an interesting game. A bowler got three tries instead of two as in tenpin bowling. And even though they had automatic pin setters with all the bells and whistles, they did not remove the deadwood after the bowler rolled his first and second ball. In fact, playing ricochets off the deadwood lying across the alley was a part of the skill of the game.

A very high score in candlepin bowling was 150-160. Nobody shot a 300 in candlepins. There were very few strikes as a matter of fact – spares were big.

The ball was between the size of a baseball and a softball. It was probably closer to the baseball than the softball.

We had a French Canadian co-worker at S.H. Brennan's Meat Packing on Broadway who got so good at candlepin bowling that he often appeared as a finalist on the TV show called *Bowling for Dollars*. On a couple of occasions, I remember going down to the Candlepin Lanes (Rec) where they filmed the show and cheering for our buddy. He would let that little ball go without a hop, skip or a jump. It would skid along the alley at 900 miles per hour. I never saw anything like it. He won often, but the prize money was no big deal – a couple of hundred dollars maybe and a free pass to Canobie Lake or some such thing.

In my mini-novel, *A Summer with Charlie*, I begin at the YMCA shooting a game of pool. I never thought that I was much of a pool player until after I left Lawrence.

I remember being at the recreation hall at boot camp in the Great Lakes. All these guys from Nebraska, Georgia, Mississippi and Idaho kept stuffing money into my pockets. They were so bad it was pathetic.

They thought that I was the greatest pool player that they had ever seen because I could draw the ball back and put some very poor right and left English on the cue ball – a little top spin also. I refused to play because most of them were so bad. But they were persistent they would come over and challenge me ... with money. Naturally I couldn't refuse. Quickly there would be a crowd around to watch.

After each guy would lose he would shake my hand in admiration like he had just been given the opportunity to shoot a game of pool with Willie Mosconi or Minnesota Fats. They would gasp to see the cue ball hit another ball and then slide backwards on the felt. They were amazed by the action of the cue ball with a top spin on it. It was a strange experience for me. I would not make the top 1000 best pool players in Lawrence, I'm sure.

I wonder why they call it English? But then Polish or Lithuanian would sound ridiculous.

There was one kid I remember who became a real champ at pool. He often played down at the Rec but he could be found at Basil's on Chestnut St. or Finno's on

Common St. or the Bowling alley and pool hall on south Broadway also called the Rec or at Rudi's on Elm and Shaw or Vic's on Jackson and Elm or the Richwood by the Common in South Lawrence.

Neither Basil's nor Finno's had a good reputation – most pool halls were not Mother approved – but as little squirts we went everywhere. I remember it cost ten cents a rack at Basil's but you had to be careful, everybody and his little brother was a hustler. I don't ever remember playing for money at Basil's or Finno's.

This kid, Billy Silva, got so good that he was backed by a bunch of local gamblers and took his act on the road like Paul Newman in the movie the Hustler. I remember him telling us some stories about his adventures and they were very similar to what went on in the movies. He quit because it got too dangerous, he told us. He had made some pretty good money but didn't feel that it was worth risking his life – or getting two broken arms.

I had my biggest hustler type experience at the Polish National on Brook St. one evening. I had finished my weight lifting workout downstairs and decided to stop at the bar for a beer or two upstairs. Well one or two beers led to four or five more and before I knew it I was shooting pool with a bunch of strangers.

This one fellow was obviously a wannabe hustler. He was buttering me up good – losing several games in a row and forfeiting his dollar gracefully. But he was so obvious. He must have thought that I was just flown in from Nebraska. He got me up to five dollars a game and, of course, I won. Finally he got all wound up and slapped a one hundred dollar bill onto the table.

"Okay, I have had it. One game! One hundred dollars, you beat me and I'm outta here."

Several people had gathered around the table. Some of them were friends of mine. My buddies were giving me the signal not to play. But it was too late for sound advice. I had downed too many beers and was shooting out of my mind. I knew this guy was hustling me but the heck with it. I had lots of money in those days. I worked three jobs and was selling meat to friends on the side. I slapped a hundred dollar bill onto the table and he flipped a coin for the right to break. We were playing Eight Ball. I won the break. I had a fantastic break, solids and strips were tumbling into the pockets. I picked high and began scooting around the table. In playing straight pool, I think I ran three racks once or twice in my life. I had occasionally run the table in eight ball but not very often.

I was shooting fast and furious; I was too drunk to know any better. I was loose as a goose. I made some of the best and most ridiculous shots that I had ever made in my life. I made a ball in the side pocket and with a little top-left I rolled the cue ball off the rail and nudged a hanger into the corner – and I called it. My opponent was smiling broadly and thumping the rubber base of his stick on the hardwood floor in appreciation after I sunk each ball. He knew I was in my glory and he was waiting for that inevitable one miss. I knew if I missed, it was all over. He would run the table like Paul Newman and be on his way with my one hundred dollar bill.

If I didn't know better myself, I would think I knew how to play position – but I didn't. Like a miracle of sorts, I just ended up behind another of my high balls after each shot. Then it happened. I left myself blind on the back rail with one ball left to sink before the eight. My last ball was sitting on the rail about to fall into the top right pocket. I couldn't go up and down. I had to go three rails through a crowd to even hit my ball. So I put a little top-left on the cue ball and punched it. My god, if I were the age I am today and in the condition that I'm am presently, I would have had a heart attack. I hit my ball perfectly. It went around the table as if it had eyes of its own. Then ... tink ... it taps my ball right in the crack between the ball and the rail after going all the way around the table. This was a once in a lifetime shot for me.

I didn't get excited though. I just looked my opponent in the eye as if this shot was something I did by habit and on a regular basis. I smirked. All his buddies started laughing.

"The hustler gets hustled," one of them choked up while laughing his butt off. All his buddies began to laugh.

But the game wasn't over yet. The eight ball was pinned against the rail about three or four inches from the side pocket. My cue ball was directly across from it on the opposite side. I had to go cross side. I had seen other guys make this shot and I had made it once or twice by accident and many other times in my dreams but ... what the hey.

I gave it a smack. The eight ball jumped off the rail and ran across the table and into the opposite side pocket.

Minnesota Fats stood there against the wall staring at me. I grabbed up the two hundred bucks, put my stick on the rack on the wall and sauntered up to the bar.

The older crowd at the bar knew me and my opponent. One guy said; "Oh my, I am so happy I came over tonight. To see somebody finally beat that son-of-a-bee is something that I will never forget. He offered to buy me a double shot of Coronet brandy – his favorite. I opted for a single shot of tequila.

Minnesota Fats left and all the gang kept buying me beers and shots of tequila. Sucking on all those damn lemons finally got to me. I don't remember where I slept that night. It could very well have been downstairs snoozing, curled up on the pressing bench, or outside in the backseat of my little, red Reno. I might not remember where I slept that night but I'll never forget that shoot out. Holy cow, I got my five minutes of fame as a $100 a game hustler. That's a pretty big deal for a Lawrence tenement dweller and ex-English Social Club pin boy.

Lawton's By the Sea

Referring to Lawton's hot dog stand at 606 Canal St. in Lawrence, Mass. as *Lawton's by the Sea* was a joke, of course. It was much the same as calling Lawrence the *Venice of America*. We did have the industrial, canal waterways that were built in the 1840's to produce cheap electrical power for the textile mills but no gondolas or Mario Lanza. We had Robert Goulet though.

The canals, along with those mammoth, redbrick mill buildings were bequeathed to the Lawrence taxpayers when the mill owners decided to take their profits and move to greener pastures and cheaper labor. I noticed in the movie *The Full Monty* the taxpayers in England were bequeathed the same type legacy. If the mill owners were required to disassemble all those redbrick mills and clean up the rivers and streams they polluted before they were allowed to leave, I'm sure they would have happily paid the workers another three cents an hour and remained in Lawrence. If that were the choice, Lawrence would still be manufacturing wool for the world.

Lawton's was there on Canal St. in the 40's, 50's and 60's when I was growing up and it was there in the late 1920's and 1930's as I understand.

It got its start catering to mill workers on their lunch break. During my day it was that place to go after a football game or victory party or a softball game under the lights at Haden Schofield Ball Park. It was especially popular when we were all a little short on cash. I think a hot dog was a quarter.

I never thought much about it at the time but years later when I had my own sandwich shop and restaurant, I remembered how Lawton's served long lines of people who showed up without warning and unannounced in no time flat. What do you do when two hundred people show up at your door and want a hot dog?

Well, Lawton's had it figured out long ago. I guess one could say that Lawton's by the Sea was a fast food joint before there was such a thing as a fast food joint. I don't know who it was that decided to just pull the dogs off the grill and throw them into the fryolator but that was a winning idea. In those days nobody was concerned about cholesterol or eating too much fat.

I remember making deliveries or pick-ups at the (Yes'um it's) Essem's hot dog plant on Beacon St. They would be mixing up the hot dogs in giant stainless steel vats. The goop in the vats would be pure white. I asked the guy working there, "What's that slop?"

"That's hot dogs," he said.

"It don't look like no hot dog that I ever saw – hot dogs are brown, man, not white."

"They'll be brown after we put the food coloring in. Before the food coloring is added, they are white. They are mostly fat."

So Lawton's would take a tube of brown, dyed fat with a little pork meat added and throw it into a fryer, probably filled with pure lard, and heat them up until the skin popped – *rippers*, they are called today. Then drop them into a toasted bun that had been drenched in butter on both sides before being slapped onto a grill. And everybody loved them. But it was all that fat that made them taste so good. Today we have skinless turkey dogs with all the fat removed, heated in a microwave oven and slapped into a dry, tasteless, cheap white bread roll – yuck! Do kids still like hot dogs today?

Hot dogs today not only don't snap, crackle or pop they are hardly worth the effort of chewing and swallowing – but they're healthier. Umm, yummy-yummy.

I remember buzzing down to Lawton's after a twilight baseball or softball game and being forced to drop two guys off with the money and our order and then circling the block a few times to pick them up because there were no places to park anywhere on Canal St. – and on both sides of the street.

You went in the door at the left side of the building. The shop was built right over the sidewalk and the darn fire hydrant was even on the inside. That was strange even in 1958. I used to really like what they called a Lobster Roll. It was a lobster salad served in one of Lawton's famous hot, buttered (on both sides) grilled hot dog rolls – and it was loaded with lobster meat. It cost considerable more than a hot dog but it was my choice when I was flush.

I never missed those grilled buttered hot dog rolls until I left Lawrence. I don't think they have those style hot dog rolls anywhere else in the United States. What I'm talking about is that style hot dog roll with bread on both sides. Hot dog rolls everywhere else are a soft crust, cheap, white bread, sub roll. You can't butter them on both sides because they don't have any sides.

When I opened my own sandwich shop in Carrabelle, Florida, I tried to duplicate Lawton's by the Sea hot dogs – in fact I tried to duplicate all my childhood sandwiches from good old Lawrence – chicken bar-b-que, Bea's veal cutlet, Italian meatball etc. The folks in the Florida Panhandle where I now live didn't even know what a meatball sandwich was. They pronounced it as if it were a dirty word and thought it to be the strangest food idea that they had ever heard. "You want me to eat a meat ...

ball sandwich? That sounds mighty nasty to me." Meatball was two words in Southern Speak.

Everybody around *these here parts* thought that I was nuts. If it wasn't rolled in cornmeal and deep fried they wouldn't eat it. I heard one comedian describe Southern cooking as deep-fried fat balls.

A big treat for a Southern boy from this area is a Moon Pie and an RC cola. A Moon Pie resembles a cream filled cake similar to what we all had as kids, except these Moon Pies are not made in a bakery; they are processed in a laboratory. I don't think they are compatible with the human digestive system. I think they just go in one end and come out the other. They are bad, man – really bad.

I have heard that Lawton's has been declared a national landmark or some such thing. Do they have park rangers working there now I wonder?

I don't know what brand of hot dog Lawton's uses today but I couldn't find a good one in 1990. Hebrew National were so filled with salt and garlic one would last a person a whole week. People told me about Siebert's brand from New York. They were poppers and had a skin on them. I watched my Southern customers remove the hot dog from the bun and peal the skin off with their fingers before they would eat them. I tried Nathan's hot dogs. My experience was that you might eat one but never two – not in the same hour anyway.

I would imagine that Lawton's used Essem brand dogs during my Lawrence tenure but after they were deep fried in lard and served in a bun slathered on both sides with real butter what difference did the brand of hot dog matter?

In today's marketplace all our meats have been dee-fatted, raised and processed under such artificial, unnatural conditions that the art of cooking has nothing to do with bringing out the natural flavors of the meats and poultry. The art of being a chef in today's world is all a matter of learning flavor-added techniques – it is injected, marinated or rubbed on.

I've been there and done all of that – from the killing tomato fields and chicken factories to sous-chef-ing French bordelaise and beurre blanc sauces. If you don't believe me, pick up a copy of *Hobo-ing America*. It is all right there in black and white – style and flavor added.

PS: I want a Lawton's old fashioned hot dog right now – and don't hold back on the fat and lard. Gimme, gimme, gimme.

Costy's Back Yard

All kids in the old neighborhood were saddled with some sort of nickname. Costy wasn't all that bad. Costy was short for Jimmy Costello. Me and Jimmy were good pals all through grade school and into high school.

The gang began accumulating in the St. Rita's schoolyard and then migrated across the street to Costy's house and back yard. Costy's house was on the corner of Exchange and Arlington.

I think my mother asked me where I was going whenever I left the house until the age of 35. My answer had an evolution. It began with; I'm goin' down to St. Rita's. Which evolved into; I'm going down to Costy's back yard or to Costy's.

Costy's evolved into; I'm goin' down to Walter's Variety. Which then dwarfed into; I'm goin' down to Nell's Variety. Then; I'm goin' up to the Howard. Which was shortened to; I'm goin' to the Corner. All of which finally arrived at; I'm goin' out.

"You're goin' out? Where?" my mother would protest.

"Just out, Ma. I'm just goin' out."

"Well who do I contact if I need you?"

"Yeah, right. Is that a trick question?"

For a period we seemed to live over at Costy's. I don't really know what the attraction was.

It may have had something to do with his cluster of attractive older sisters. Jimmy had four big sisters.

Let's see if I can remember their names? There was the oldest, Carol. She was very tall. Next in line was Betty. I think we considered Betty as the wild one. Next came Pat. She was the Maureen O'Hara of the group. A real knockout as I remember with long, curly red hair, freckles and the works. Mike was the youngest. I think her real name was Marlene. But everyone called her Mike. She was the closest to our age and was therefore not to be admired or gawked over.

We would hang around and play at Costy's all day long, seven days a week. You would think that we would have driven his parents nuts. But I guess they just loved kids.

Mrs. Costello was active in the church and at the school. She cooked lunches over at St. Rita's for the kids who had to be bussed in. She baked cookies and cakes for all the special fund raisers at the Immaculate Conception Church. She was busy, busy, busy.

I remember her bringing the whole bunch of us pitchers of Kool-Aid and popping us popcorn. She was a real sweetheart.

We rarely transgressed into the homes of our buddies, but Costy's house was always open.

I remember sitting in their living room waiting for Jimmy one afternoon or early evening. The Nelson Family was on the TV. Little, wise cracking Ricky was growing up. He was busting into teenager-hood. He debuted his first rock recording on the show that evening. He sang, played the guitar and did a little twisting or fancy footwork or whatever – a little imitation Elvis, thought us boys. The Costello sisters, on the contrary, went bonkers. Me and Jimmy grumbled and shook our heads as we walked out the door listening to screeches and different refrains of *he's so cute*. We were totally disgusted by the whole display. We liked little, Ricky as he was – little, skinny, unattractive and wisecracking.

We played in Costy's back yard, in the streets and on the sidewalks that framed in Costy's house. As I remember there were neighborhood little girls that were playing around the area also.

One little cutie came to town visiting from some far off distant land like New Jersey or New York. She was the bell of the hopscotch squares for her entire visit. I would guess she never got so much little boy attention in all her life. All the boys had a crush on her. I actually found myself taking special note of this young lady also.

I had flashed her *the look* on several occasions and sauntered by, exhibiting my best Brando indifference. I truly felt that things were moving along in the proper direction. She was speaking to me and smiling and all the rest. Finally one day, she came bumping up to me all big eyed and friendly-like.

"Could I talk to you?" she asked coyly. I was, of course, ready. I just knew she was harboring a thing for me.

"Sure," I said.

"Do you think Jimmy likes me?" she asked.

After a very long disappointing pause, I grunted ... and said, not very nicely. "How would I know? Why don't you ask him?"

"Would you ask him for me?" she persisted, ignoring my bad attitude completely.

"Would I ask Jimmy if he likes you?"

"Ah huh, and then when he tells you, maybe you could tell me what he says."

This was a rather strange game that I had never played before. Why would I do this? I would do this because of those large, searching eyes staring up at me ... helpless, yearning, desirous, longing – but all for Jimmy Costello. God, where would I file this bit of disappointment in my photographic memory book? Right under having my bike stolen or being beat up by Joyce Bouchard, a girl. How the hell does one guy ask another guy if he likes a particular girl without seeming like a complete putz head.

"Hey Jimmy, do you like Little Lulu?"

"What's it to ya? You writin' a book?"

"Ahhh ..."

"Sure, I like her, doesn't everybody? What are you crazy? She's beautiful. She's a doll. She's something else."

"Yeah, well, she asked me to ask you if you liked her."

"She did? Well, tell her yes. Sure I do! Wow! I can't believe it. Go ahead and tell; and tell me what she says then."

"Wait a minute! Wait a minute. I ain't running back and forth with little love messages here. What am I, the Good Fairy? This game could go on forever. How about this? Now that you know that she likes you, how about you just going up to her and ... and ... whatever. Say something to her."

"Like what?"

"I don't know like what. That's your damn problem."

"Well you don't have to get all pissy about it."

"I ain't getting pissy."

"Oh, you're not? Sounds pretty pissy to me."

"Look, I'm done here. You're on your own."

"Thanks a bunch."

"You're welcome."

I remember observing them both rather bitterly as they hopped each other's scotch gleefully on the sidewalk in front of Costy's house. I thought it to be rather disgusting, as I remember.

I don't remember why we left Costy's back yard but I think the gang kept growing. There were a lot of kids in that Arlington neighborhood and we just kept piling up and piling up in Costy's back yard. Something had to give.

But Jimmy Costello's back yard and Mr. and Mrs. Costello and all the Costello sisters and little Eddy,

Jimmy's younger brother, all remain prominent in my large book of memories. And a very good memory they all are – very Irish too.

Appropriately, I don't even remember that little, New Jersey girl's name. Let's just call her Jezebel.

Somebody's Got to Lose

"Well Richie, somebody has got to win and somebody has got to lose." This was my favorite uncle's philosophical chant after my big brother, Ernie and his team, lost a game at the Central Catholic Auditorium.

It was always Ernie and his team to me. All the other guys on the court were just there staying out of my big brother's way and assisting every now and then in another of his victories. And he was a *big* brother at six foot four inches tall. I would say that my brother Ernie was the best basketball player ever to play for Central Catholic High School in Lawrence but it would be much more acceptable to say that he was my favorite CCHS basketball star. I was extremely proud to be dubbed *little Ernie* by the big guys who played at the St. Rita's schoolyard and chose me to fill in one of their choose-up games.

My favorite uncle, Ray Essick, just didn't realize how close he came to being strangled to death each and every time he came out with that sing-song refrain of his. "Well, Richie, somebody has got to win and somebody has got to lose."

I could have just killed him. My response was equally repetitive but much more emotional.

"I know that Uncle Ray ... but it is supposed to be the OTHER team that loses, not Ernie's team."

My uncle would laugh as he drove along in his 1949, black Pontiac and later in his 1956, prized, Dodge, automatic, push-button drive.

My Uncle Ray was meticulous when it came to his automobiles. Well, he was rather meticulous about everything: his pointy leather shoes; his felt, dress-up hats; his eating habits; his bookkeeping; his suits and ties, his colorful winter sweaters; his postal clerk's job – just about everything, I guess.

I always felt that my Uncle Ray missed his calling in life. Instead of a postal clerk, he should have been a school teacher – a grade school teacher. He had a unique ability when it came to the *little people.*

Whenever I would stumble up beside him no matter what he was doing – wood working, shoe shining, ledger keeping, filling an oil squirt can, whatever – he would immediately start instructing me in the intricacies of that trade. To my Uncle Ray everything was important, whether it be licking an envelope and sealing it properly or building concrete steps on the old homestead at 32 Chelmsford St.

He taught me how to ride a bicycle, change a flat bicycle tire and how to lick an ice cream cone properly. He also taught me the proper technique for eating a juicy, rather sloppy, Bea's chicken bar-b-que sandwich.

I invariably remember his lean-forward-over-the-plate technique just after I slop a blob of something onto my clean, white shirt. Each time it happens today, I see my Uncle Ray standing there next to me, as clear as day, smiling and shaking his head. I have even resorted to his napkin stuffed in the shirt collar trick but always after the damage has been done. Stupid is a difficult thing to conquer. It has always been one of my bigger challenges.

I must admit that there were occasions when I found his meticulousness a bit trying. For example, Uncle Ray's proper method for shoveling snow. Come on?

Well anyway, one should never attempt to scoop up more than a half shovelful of snow. One must mark off a half shovelful in the deep snow by sticking his shovel into the drift and outlining the chosen area with slits made by poking the shovel into the snow. Then insert shovel and extract the proper amount of snow. Then do not throw the snow over one's shoulder; no, no, no. Carry the half shovel of snow over to the fence and place it there to create a proper pile. Throwing the snow over your shoulder only served to clean one area while cluttering another.

I know Uncle Ray was right. But when your ten years old and have more energy than brains, the over the shoulder method seemed twice as fast even if it was not all that efficient.

He had a method for everything. Every encounter with Uncle Ray was a lesson of one type or another.

My Uncle Ray was the youngest in his family. He lived with his mother until he was well into his forties. I think he was forty-eight years old when he decided to get married. Then all hell broke loose. Very soon thereafter he had a set of twins and then a little girl.

I never realized it until I was grown and got into reading books but it seems back in those days one child in all immigrant families was assigned the task of caring for mom and dad. It was often the youngest child on whom this burden fell. I don't know if that is why my Uncle Ray held off to his late forties to get married but it could very well have been the case.

I wasn't particularly crazy about my favorite uncle's choice in a bride but to be quite honest, I never liked any of his girlfriends. He would often introduce them to me and ask, "Well Richie, how would you like Abigail here or Eleanor for a new aunt?" My response was usually rather crude, like, "I don't need any more aunts. I have enough now already."

I remember one redheaded, bombshell of my uncle's grabbing hold of my little cheek and pinching it so hard, I thought she had pulled half my face off before she finished with her, "Oh, aren't you a little darling." Her smile said *little darling* but her pinch said otherwise. She made her point though. But nevertheless, I didn't find her any more appealing as a possible aunt.

I always felt my uncle had his hands full with his new bride and his blossoming family. I was getting older. I had my friends out on the corner and my uncle and I drifted apart but occasionally we spoke and I kept an eye on him.

I remember one day watching him huffing and puffing down the street holding the back of a bicycle seat while one of his kids was learning the bike riding ropes. The little kid did just as I had. She kept screaming "don't let go" and when she peeked over her shoulder and saw that Uncle Ray had let go, the front wheel suddenly went bonkers and she went crashing into the curb and fell down. Just as with me, my uncle laughed uproariously. I had to chuckle at the older, gray haired guy out in the middle of Chelmsford St. still teaching some little kid how to ride a bike and still getting the greatest of laughs over the whole deal.

Then one day came the finale. I was walking down the street and my uncle pulled up beside me in his newest, new car.

"Where you goin', Richie? Hop in."

I strolled over to the car and opened the door. Two tonic (pop, soda) bottles rolled out and tumbled to the ground. As they rolled around on the asphalt and I scurried around to gather them up other debris came tumbling out, a couple of empty potato chip bags and an empty Good & Plenty container as I remember. This wouldn't have been all that shocking except that it was the new car of my meticulous, favorite Uncle Ray. I said, "Ah, you never heard of a litterbag."

"Richie," he said slightly heated but still smiling. "A man has got to do what a man has to do. Things are a little less organized these days but we're dealing with it as best we can."

"Yes, I suppose," I said. "You know, somebody has got to win and somebody has got to lose."

"Pardon me," he said, snatching some napkins and a half eaten hot dog from the dashboard and throwing it under his seat. "What was that, Richie?"

"How's everything going? Looks like the wife and kids are getting a little ahead of you?" I asked.

"Well Richie, life is a matter of adapting. We do what we have to do and we try to keep everything peaceful. You know what I mean."

"Are you having any regrets with this later life family and all?"

"Not really, Richie. It's hectic and things run differently but you know, I think the kids are keeping me young. I feel I got to stay young just to keep up with them." And then he laughed.

What he said seemed strange to me because I remembered him when his hair was black and not gray. I remembered him when he looked like somebody's boyfriend and not somebody's father or grandfather. I remembered him when he was as neat as a pin.

But even then, in that cluttered car with the candy wrappers and the pop bottles and the loose paper all over the front seat, he was still quite a guy – a very admirable fellow, I thought. He was living his life and he was adapting and loving and laughing all the while. He was a philosopher and he was a teacher. He was still providing me with instruction. He certainly wasn't one of the losers in this life. He was a winner all the way to the finish. I feel very lucky to have had an Uncle Ray in my life. He is now, and always will be, one of my fondest memories.

The Merry Mac Club
Frankie and Johnnie were Sweethearts

The Merry Mac Club up on the River Road became the place to go for several years. On weekends and Tuesday's Talent Night, it was packed – standing room only.

The owner hired local bands to play on the weekends and Tuesday's Talent Night was a spectacle. There were a few talented people who showed up every once and awhile but for most, it was a laugh and dare type thing. I suppose it was like the Karaoke of today. The audience loved to boo and scream and make fun of the volunteers. Every now and then someone like my buddy Peter Shaheen would slide in between one horror show or another. Peter was an excellent vocalist, boarding on the professional. He would slip onto the stage; start singing and the whole place would quiet down as everyone turned to one another and said, "My god, where did they find that guy?" But other than Peter and one or two others it was just for laughs. And it was a lot of laughs. People loved Tuesday nights at the Merry Mac Club.

But the weekends were jumping also. Most nights it was two and three deep at the bar. Barstools were at a premium. I was there at the bar with a couple of my buddies every weekend and Tuesday nights all winter long.

We were, of course, getting in shape, pumping up and working towards our professional alcoholic's status. We were registry eligible but not officially certified at that particular point in time. A few more evening classes at the Seagram's Institute for Mumbling and some extra credit courses at the Smirnoff Clinic for Advanced Obnoxiousness where one learned to control slurring and make stumbling and spit spraying in conversation appear impromptu and accidental, were all we had left. Then we would get our licenses and be able to practice professionally in any barroom in America.

The owner was a tall, large man. He ate well. I know because he bought a lot of his meat at my little butcher shop. He was a good customer of mine ... as I was of his. He spent a few hundred dollars with me every month. He would buy whole pork loins and whole ribs and loins that I would custom cut for him.

He was a very nice fellow, rather quiet, I thought. He had a girlfriend. She was also very quiet. She was a cute little thing. I remember her very well – and you will know why in just a minute.

She had been working for the owner for a long time. She had a title. She was the bar manager or some such thing. She was petit, with shiny black hair. She was not showy or brash. She was friendly but not excessively so. She was very pretty. She was there all the time. Sometimes I would stop in before the crowd came and pull up a seat next to her at the bar and shoot the breeze and tease her. She was a good laugher.

Unfortunately the owner had a wife also ... but really this was not all that unusual for local bar owners ... or for local anybodies. It sometimes seemed to me that there were more married men out on the prowl in those days than there were single guys. It was a rather common practice. The fact that this particular bar owner had a girlfriend was nothing surprising or out of the ordinary. I never even thought about it.

Until one day my petit little girlfriend/barmaid came walking into the club when the boss was behind the bar.

She called out his name and when he turned she lifted a revolver from her side and started firing.

Some of my friends happened to be there that afternoon and they told me what transpired. They were diving from their stools and taking cover. They peeked out from behind a tipped over tiny, drink table and waited until she stopped shooting.

I lost a good customer that afternoon. I heard that my cute, little conversation partner emptied her revolver into her ex-boyfriend. They had had a disagreement. It seems that he wanted to have an even more open relationship than they were sharing at the time. He had another girl that he wanted to see. He did. But he neglected to talk it over with girlfriend number one, the bar manager. She obviously felt that this was a more serious infraction on their relationship than he was aware of.

When I recall this story I always think of that song *Frankie and Johnnie were Sweethearts*. I've never been able to get the story out of my mind. It all seemed so impossible. She was so attractive. Why didn't she just find somebody else? What was she so upset about? She was dating a married man after all. If she took cheating so seriously, what about her boyfriend's wife and kids? Did she ever think about what her relationship with her boss was doing to his wife's psychological development? Did she really think that he would divorce his wife, abandon his children, give up his home, his life's work and a good part of his acquired wealth to run off with her? How do you figure it?

Sometimes when I tell this story, I conclude by suggesting that one must be careful when engaging in relationships. Some take their involvements more seriously than others. But I know that there is more to a story like this than that simple evaluation. This is the stuff of a novel if I ever wanted to get into it. But I doubt that I ever will.

After she emptied her revolver, she pulled up a stool and set her gun on the bar. "Somebody call the police," I was told she said, matter-of-factly.

She sat there quietly and waited until the cops arrived. There was no question about her being convicted. She went to prison. And that's all I know.

I guess what has always bothered me about this story is that all the participants were regular folks. As far as I could tell, they were all normal everyday people. They laughed; they joked; they worked. The murdered club owner shopped at my market. I cut his pork chops, ground his hamburger and wrapped his porterhouse steaks. The murderess mixed my drinks. I talked and joked with her.

Didn't she have a buddy or a girlfriend she could talk to? I always wished she would have asked me about it. I'm sure I could have thought of a better idea.

It was such a sad story, a very sad story. And, in my opinion, it was all so unnecessary ... so totally unnecessary.

Big Town – Small Town

I spent approximately half my life growing up in a big city, Lawrence, Massachusetts and the other half here in the small town of Eastpoint, Florida. There were probably more people in a one mile radius of my original tenement apartment in Essex County than there is in the entire Franklin County. I thought it would be interesting to compare the two areas and the lifestyles.

Both of my hometowns were/are poor communities. I understand that the residents in either of these hometowns take offence at being classified as poor. But if the historical record of either community is checked, the facts belie the opinions and prejudices of the residents. I don't know the present status of Franklin County but any record book that I have looked into will show Franklin County historically as among the poorest counties in Florida. My other hometown, Lawrence, is and has been one of the poorest cities in America since the late 1880s.

The residents of either of my hometowns will claim that money or per capita income is not everything. There are other values and qualities that make their respective communities worthwhile and even better and happier than places that boast of more money and greater prosperity. I agree. If I didn't I wouldn't have remained in this community for the past 30 years.

Both communities were/are poor. I point this out to make note that poverty has different faces. I have no doubt that if all the poor living in Franklin County were shipped up to my first hometown, in the Merrimack Valley, they would crawl all the way back to the poverty of Franklin County rather than to try and exist in the poverty of that big city. There is a big difference between being small town, country poor and being big city, ghetto poor.

I'm sure if I took photographs showing the basic poverty of both communities and published each in the opposing community's local newspapers, both towns would recognize the squalor of the other while seeing nothing unusual about their own. It's the old frog in the heating water, syndrome.

Comparing the politics is also interesting. I know that people in Franklin County are often frustrated by their local politics. They scream corruption, nepotism, wasteful spending and a lack of transparency. In the big city the corruption is amplified a thousand times, nepotism and job favoritism is everywhere and the lack of transparency borders on the invisible.

In the small town much of the local news travels around by word of mouth – a little card on the post office door. In the big city a little card on the post office door probably wouldn't even be read by the busy postmaster.

Traditionally both the small town and the big city depended on area and local newspapers for their regional information. Local newspapers were once a very important source of information for the small town and the big city alike. Things are changing.

In my old hometown there was a local newspaper that was started in the 1860's. It has a rich archive of local historical lore. Today that local newspaper, I have been told, is owned by a rich millionaire or billionaire who owns and operates a chain of newspapers around the nation. My old hometown was an industrial, mill town.

The American industrial revolution began in the area. The town was established in 1840 and it was built around a textile mill. In fact, it was settled and populated in preparation for the mill and the manufacturing. It was a heavy blue-collar, worker community with strong union roots and traditions. One of the biggest labor strikes in U.S. history took place there in 1912. It was called the *Bread and Roses Strike*.

The paper which was locally owned for over a century and published to reflect the neighborhood and the city's local values is now owned by a man who was born and raised in South Carolina (that's better than China, I suppose). A man, I have been told, who has little sincere interest in the local values or in many of the differing communities. I am told that he is there promoting his personal propaganda. He covers his editorial opinions with a light sprinkling of local color.

The newspaper business in Franklin County is the same. The one local newspaper finally sold out to a giant media manipulator. The local paper is heavily slanted to the right, as would be expected. Poor folk don't own newspapers.

I worked for a number of years for an area-grown, small town media man. He lost more in the 15 years that he ran the newspaper than I earned in my lifetime.

Why did he do it? He had amassed a small fortune in his lifetime – mostly inheritance – and he used the newspaper as a tax write-off. It is interesting to note that even though the paper was a tax write-off, he still wouldn't pay his reporters and writers more than the minimum wage and no travel expenses – not even gas money. If a writer wanted to submit a commentary, if accepted, it was FREE. The writer's only reward existing in the glory of publication – the ransom of ... a by-line.

Relationships with neighbors and making friends, is also interesting to compare.

I am still in regular contact with many of my old neighborhood friends – friends that I made in grade school, playing in the streets and hanging out on the street corners. The internet and the e-mail have helped out enormously in that regard.

Most of my buddies are in agreement that the friends they established in their childhood in the old neighborhood remain their closest personal relationships other than immediate family members, of course.

I find that somewhat interesting. One of my buddies who was very successful and well traveled confessed to me that his childhood buddies are still the ones he thinks most about. He considered most of the people that he met since leaving the old neighborhood, whether in business or neighbors, only acquaintances – some close acquaintances but acquaintances nonetheless. I'm in the same boat, sorta.

I made lifelong friends growing up in my old hometown and I think of one or another of them every day. But I was very happy to leave Lawrence and I don't want to go back. To the contrary, I've enjoyed my years here in Franklin Country, friendless as it is.

But to be truthful, I would much rather be parked in a motorhome or travel trailer somewhere in Oregon, Oklahoma, Texas, Michigan or anywhere – not knowing a soul. Small town or big town, I enjoyed the life of a vagabond/hobo best of all. There is something confining and restricting about living anywhere permanently. The more you know, the worse it gets – and I don't read newspapers.

Good Old Dr. Lemmings, the Friendly Dentist

When it comes to braces, I'm pretty much a bigot. I see so many little kids walking around with braces today I wonder if they are not a part of a new and strange pandemic. Do these things just grow on kids' teeth today? Certainly the average American working family can't afford all this steel framing? When we were kids, acne was the big problem. Today it's shrapnel. It grows on their teeth, out of their ears, noses, eyelids and belly buttons.

"When I was a kid nobody had braces in my Lawrence neighborhood. We couldn't afford the basics, never mind the eye wash," boasted Richard Edward Noble time and time again from his pompous I-was-poorer-than-you class status. "I remember kids with missing teeth, overgrown front teeth, buck teeth, chipped front teeth, bad teeth, crooked teeth, yellowed teeth and rotted teeth ... but no damn braces! What, are you going to be a movie star? You think you're going to grow up to be Rock Hudson or Miss America or something? A cap is something you wear to a baseball game and a filling is that stuff they put in jelly donuts. Are you kidding me, dentists and braces in Lawrence?"

But you know what? I completely forgot about my buddy Russ Brown. How could I ever have forgotten Russ? I went with him to Dr. Lemmings' office after school two or three times a week for two years, I think.

I remember sitting in Dr. Lemmings' office up on Broadway reading his out of date magazines for hour after hour. I could hear all the drilling and buzzing. That smell, I'll never forget it. I guess it was burning teeth enamel. Yuck, they'll never get me into one of them dentist chairs.

And I can proudly say that I went to the dentist only once in my life. The inside of my mouth can pass inspection in any third world country. My wife has already made the excursion to Affordable Dentures and now I'm next. One day service; in and everything is out.

I can still see my wife coming out of that office at Affordable Dentures – teeth free. I never felt so guilty in my life. Her mouth all swollen and filled with cotton, blood dribbling down both sides her chin. She looked like she had just been beaten in the back alley behind the Old Horse Shoe Bar on Park St.

I took her for a milkshake. She tried to drink it but with all the Novocain in her gums, it just wouldn't work. She sucked and sucked but everything came dribbling out the sides. I said, "For god's sakes swallow. Don't just spit it out!"

She said, "Blubber dubberr, mah mah, wha wha."

I said, "First suck, then close your mouth and put your head back and swallow."

She said, "Mama blubber dubber fubber foo." And she said it loudly and with heated enthusiasm. I instinctively knew that she was not happy. Of course, there was no reason for her to be talking to me in that tone of voice, with or without any teeth, but I realized that she was under some stress. I let it go; after all, I had no idea what the hell she was blubbering about anyway.

I told her to remember, "This shall also pass." That is one of my favorite lines. I use it quite often. But in this case she swung her left arm, hit me in the chest and knocked my French fries all over me. It was lucky I hadn't put any ketchup on them yet.

I said, "Just because you can't eat, that is no reason to smack my French fries all over hell. I bought you a milk shake didn't I?"

She said ... actually it was more like a scream, "Flubber foo! Foo flubbering fit nit. Flow and flobb your phelff you pphrogging forron."

About two weeks later and after she had downed nine hundred cups of beef and chicken broth, I entered the living room. She was sitting in her chair sobbing with her new teeth in her hand. Carol doesn't sob very often. I was very surprised. "What's wrong?"

"I'm never going to be able to eat again," she gummed with lips flapping in a Moms Mabley fashion.

She looked so pathetic, I had to laugh.

She glared.

I said, after thinking for a moment or two. "This shall also pass."

She looked up at me with hate and a viciousness that I had never seen before in all our married life. I thought I had seen every bad look that she had in her repertoire – but obviously, I was mistaken.

This shall also pass didn't make the grade for this situation. I needed something better. I said, "Carol, we have been married a long time and I know you pretty well by now. If there is one thing I know for sure about you, it is that no matter what the obstacle, you will figure out a way to eat. I have no doubt."

For a second, I thought she might smile; it didn't happen. But, today she is once again eating – thank you Fix-a-dent.

I was in my early twenties when I made my one and only visit to a dentist. I had something growing in my mouth. It was another tooth. It was killing me and had been killing me for days. Me and my buddy Dutch were walking down Broadway and I spotted Dr. Lemmings' sign in the second floor of one of the office buildings. I remembered going there with Russ. I decided that it was time for me to bite the bullet. I didn't want to do it but Dutch insisted.

I crawled up the old wooded steps to Doctor Lemmings' office reluctantly. Dutch was behind me, prodding, pushing and offering words of encouragement.

It didn't help. We were now on the second floor landing. There were a couple of offices. The door to Dr. Lemmings' office was open. We slipped in. There was no receptionist. Things must have been going downhill for Dr. Lemming. His office was now one room. There was a Dentist chair with all the horrible paraphernalia hanging around it, like out of some science fiction movie. It was next to the window. It had a fold out, multi-colored, artificial cardboard, wall thingie hiding it. Like those things they have at a Chinese restaurant. There was an old coffee table with some magazines on it and three dusty, much used, very uncomfortable looking chairs up against the wall behind the coffee table.

Dr. Lemming was not around. I suggested that we leave. Dutch suggested that we sit down and wait. "Maybe he just stepped out for a minute," he said.

We sat down. I picked up a magazine. The magazines were older than the ones I remembered reading when I had visited his much bigger, neater office back in the days of Russ Brown and his junior high braces. There was a *Time* magazine with a picture of Adolf Hitler on the cover. I showed it to Dutch. *Germany Surrenders*, Dutch said, reading the caption on the cover. "Well it is certainly about time. I was beginning to think that they never would. I wonder if Hirohito has given up the old Shinto temple yet?"

"I don't think so. I think he's still hiding out in some jungle on Guam or on the shores of Iwo Jima someplace."

"Yeah, well I'm sure they will get him one of these days."

"Good afternoon boys. Can I help somebody?" asked this little, old, gray haired man in a white coat holding a cup of coffee. He was a lot older. His back was humping and he appeared much shorter than I remembered.

"No," I said. "We just stopped in to catch up on the news. Let's go Dutch."

"He's got a sore tooth," Dutch said nodding in my direction.

"Well let's take a look at it," Igor said, pointing over to the electric chair.

He poked around in my mouth and then announced that it was a wisdom tooth that was causing all the problem. I then suggested that maybe I ought to hang onto anything in my body that related to wisdom.

"It is up to you," answered Dr. Lemming.

"Oh well, I've got this far, maybe you ought to pull it out."

"Out it is," said Dr. Lemming, slapping his hands together and rubbing them eagerly. "Let's shoot you up with a little Novocain and we'll have that baby out in no time."

He pulled out a needle that looked more like a turkey baster. Oh God!

He shot me up and then went over to where Dutch was sitting. He picked up his coffee and began chatting with Dutch.

"Looks like rain."

"Could be."

"You don't smoke, do ya?"

"No."

"Me neither. I just quit. Of course, if you happened to have a cigarette, I would have joined you in a smoke."

"No, I don't smoke."

"Does your buddy, smoke?"

"I think he does."

"You got a smoke on you there, buddy?" Dr. Lemming yelled to me over in the electric chair.

"I ddrew, bub I domt haph benny om me."

"Ah huh! Sounds like he is about ready, don't it?"

"It sure does."

The Doctor then picked up what looked to be a pair of heavy duty vice grips. I couldn't believe it.

"Now don't worry you won't feel a thing. You will feel some pressure but no pain."

He clamped the vice grips down onto my tooth and then began to pull.

I could hear what sounded like a tree limb cracking. I felt pressure – a lot of damn pressure. Igor struggled and struggled. There was a good deal of creaking and crunching noises.

"Jesus Christ, that damn tooth is really in there," Dr. Lemming squeezed out between his clenched teeth as he grimaced and struggled harder and now with both hands. "I need to get some leverage here." He climbed up onto the side of the electric chair. He struggled for a bit but then determined that he needed a little better angle. "I am going to have to ask you to give me a little help here. I ain't as young as I used to be. I'm going to put one knee on your chest here to get a bit more leverage. Then I'm going to give it hell. When I start pulling, you put your both hands here on my chest and push. Maybe between the both of us we can get this sucker."

The Doctor had both hands on the vice grips, his left foot on the side of the electric chair and his right knee on my chest.

This all began to appear questionable to me. Number one: How did he know he had the right tooth? Number two: If my tooth was stuck into my head this tight, maybe we shouldn't be trying to pull it out? Number three: Did I tell him to pull it out or did he tell me? If it was me that told him, why the hell was he listening to me? I'm no dentist. Number four: Was he really Doctor Lemming the dentist, or had he just wandered in from attending the coffee shop and decided to make himself a fast thirty bucks?

I could just see Dutch out of the corner of my right eye. His eyes were open very, very wide. His body was upright and rigid and his hands were braced on the arms of his chair as if he were on an airplane that was descending rapidly – possibly to his death. I began questioning my decision further. I decided that I had to get this crazy bastard off me and get the hell out of there.

I gave the Doctor a strong push with both my hands. I heard a ripping, crunching noise coming from my mouth as the Doctor went tumbling off the chair. When he hit the floor he was stumbling backwards in a rapid tripping motion. Dutch leaped from his seat and grabbed hold of the old buck before he tumbled back onto his ass.

I sat up in my chair. I looked at Dutch with the doctor cradled in his arms. Dutch looked frightened.

"Look a here," screamed Dr. Lemmings as he held his vice grips with my extracted wisdom tooth clasped between its jaws up into the air. "We got that sucker!" he shouted gleefully. "I'm gonna have to start exercising a little more. That one almost got the best of me."

Yes, that was my first and last trip to a dentist's office.

Interesting to note about forty years later, I returned to Lawrence for a reunion with the old gang. The first one to greet me was Russ Brown. He slapped me on the back and shot me a beaming smile. "Well, look at those teeth," I said. "Those are the biggest, shiniest teeth I've ever seen on a white man. I guess all those trips to Dr. Lemmings' office paid off after all."

"Are you kidding," he said, slipping his fingers into his mouth and pulling out all his lowers. That crazy bugger drilled every tooth in my damn head. I had to have everything pulled out before I was forty. I've had false teeth for over twenty years now."

Good old Dr. Lemming, the friendly Lawrence dentist.

Books by Richard Edward Noble

Hobo-ing America
A Summer with Charlie
Honor Thy Father and Thy Mother
The Eastpointer
A Little Something
Noble Notes on Famous Folks
A Baker's Dozen
Just Hangin' Out, Ma
America on Strike
Mein Kampf – Analysis of Book One

These books are available on the internet at the major vending sites. Bookstores, libraries and other vendors can contact Noble Publishing:

richardedwardnoble@fairpoint.net

or

Noble Publishing,
box 643,
Eastpoint, Florida 32328
for volume discounts.

HOBO-ING AMERICA

Seeing the U.S.A. clinging to the elbow of Carol and Dick will be an awakening for most Americans no matter how many times they have toured the U.S.A.

Come along with Carol and Dick and live in the places where Charles Kuralt was afraid to park his bus.

Feel the pain, joy and anger and shake the calloused hands that make America what it is.

See America in its glory and its shame. See it from the highways, the sidewalks and the gutters. Meet Asians, Indians, Jamaicans, Haitians, Mexicans. Meet most of them in one chicken factory in central Arkansas on the third shift.

See America from the bottom of the cracker barrel. Come along with Carol and Dick. Talk to the *Crackers* and fill the barrels.

A SUMMER WITH CHARLIE

A Summer with Charlie will make you laugh.
A Summer with Charlie will make you cry.
This is one of those stories that is supposed to make you cry. If you read it and you don't cry you're a better man than I am, Charlie Brown! This is a short story, but it tags all the bases. It deals with the *big stuff*. It deals with life, love, morality, sex, death, religion, friendship, boys and girls, growing up, home, neighborhood and country. For me it is a trip down memory lane. It's the old days, the old places and the old gang. Despite the seriousness of the subject matter, it is a story of memories, youth and laughter.

HONOR THY FATHER AND THY MOTHER

Honor Thy Father and Thy Mother is a tragic novel. The main character is a little boy. The reader learns to understand Richard by listening to his thoughts. We read his mind as he tries to make sense of those around him. We follow Richard's thoughts from ages five to thirteen as he translates the people, the circumstances, and the society around him. The reader will walk through a tragedy of personal, religious and social confusion. Anyone who reads this book will be left with some very difficult impressions and many shocking images that will never go away.

The book is an attempt to distinguish between discipline and abuse, between a spanking and a beating, between being scolded and being harried, between learning and indoctrination. It is a journey through the rational and the irrational.

Honor Thy Father and Thy Mother is also a love story and it is a study in the nature of hate at the same time. It is about family and religion. It is about hard times and depression. It is about alcohol and alcoholism. It is about what is going on in the apartment upstairs or the tenement next door. It is real life – and death.

THE EASTPOINTER

My column *the Eastpointer* appeared each week in the Franklin Chronicle. In 2007 I won the first place award for humor from the Florida Press Association.

Eastpoint is in the Florida Panhandle, across the bridge from Apalachicola to the west and a few miles from the town of Carrabelle to the east. All three of these small communities are located in Franklin County on the Gulf Coast.

Franklin County has been, traditionally a seafood community. This volume contains a selection of columns that not only present the ideas and opinions of the author but create a portrait of life in the *sleepy, little fishing village* of Eastpoint. These stories are intended to be fun, entertaining and stimulate a laugh here and there. Hopefully they also contain a bit of wisdom along with the chuckles.

A LITTLE SOMETHING

A Little Something is a volume of poetry with prose. The volume is divided into several categories – My Hometown, Humor, Love and Other Nice Things, Tenderness and Tears, and On the Serious Side. The poetry is traditional in style and, as with all poetry, covers a wide range of interests and ideas.

BUT, DO YOU LOVE ME

But, do you love me?
And how would I know?
I look into your eyes, but the love doesn't show.
So how ... how would I know?
Days and nights, weeks and years,
Moments of laughter, and a lifetime of tears.

But do you love me?
And how would I know?
Nothing I see would tell me it's so.
We touch, we love, we laugh, we smile.
We cherish the moments, mile after mile.

But do you love me?
And how would I know?
Unless once in a while...
You'd tell me so.

NOBLE NOTES ON FAMOUS FOLKS

Noble Notes on Famous Folks was intended to be informative but yet entertaining – hopefully even humorous. I had great fun writing this book. I would like to do two or three more like it.

I was inspired to write a book in this style by stumbling onto a writer by the name of Willy Cuppy. Mr. Cuppy wrote a number of great books. His most famous is probably, *The Rise and Fall of Practically Everybody*.

My book states the basic facts of the people it describes with usually some not so well known tidbits thrown in. Many of the famous characters described in these pages are funny with no additional elaboration. There have been some really strange famous people – Abelard, Francis Bacon, and Tycho Brahe to point out just a few.

There are some who have stories that most people just wouldn't believe. For example: Archimedes, Alexander the Great, Walt Whitman, and even Charles Lindbergh. If you like history, you will love this book. If you don't like history because it is too dull and often written boringly, you will love this book. If you would like to read something and maybe learn a little something at the same time, this book is for you. Try it. I really think you will like it.

A BAKER'S DOZEN

When I write about things that are common to my wife Carol and me, her comment is, "I love reading my husband's descriptions of our adventures. I get the enjoyment from the adventure I experienced and then the added pleasure of reading about the trip he went on." I guess I have been on a *trip* all my life.

All the stories in this book happened. They just may not have happened exactly as I have described them.

Big Jim was quite a man, a local hero to us kids. Cain and Bernard's barroom was the real thing. We all loved Walter, of Walter's Variety Store. Jeannie was the prettiest thing I had ever seen. Poor, little Howie, Gluckman with his gooey cigar, and Billy with his butcher's cleaver, I will never forget any of them.

JUST HANGIN' OUT MA

Thank God for the street corners of Lawrence, Mass. and being able to hang out. I started writing stories about the gang and hangin' out when I was eighteen years old. Then life came along and got in my way. Now I'm back. As far as I'm concerned, I'm stronger and better equipped to do justice to the old gang and the street corners that made hangin' out so memorable.

These anecdotes cover more than just the variety stores, drugstores and street corners of my youth. They branch out into barrooms, nightclubs, poolrooms, bowling alleys and the Full Monty of the *I'm Just Hangin' Out, Ma* experience.

I hope you all enjoy these escapades, feel the love, get the jokes, and have some laughs.

AMERICA ON STRIKE

If you don't know the History of American Labor, you don't know American History

I have come to the conclusion that the labor movement in America and around the world is the key to understanding or misunderstanding modern history. It is the Rosetta Stone to deciphering modern day politics.

The descendents of the Holocaust victims rewrite their story anew every generation vowing that it shall never be forgotten. It is the obligation of each generation to rewrite the past in the vocabulary of their times in order to keep it alive for all time.

This book is my small contribution to keeping the worker history of America alive for another generation.

MEIN KAMPF—ANALYSIS OF BOOK ONE

Who are the American Nazis? The Democrats or the Republicans?

Adolf Hitler was a self-styled messiah, preaching a faith. He came from out the Germanic woods like the fabled Siegfried to rescue his people from world domination.

World War I and Adolf Hitler's experiences as a soldier played a key role in shaping his radical personality and moral judgments.

Everything that confronts us today in our political debate is and was debated in *Mein Kampf*.

Analysing Adolf Hitler has certainly been an experience. Unfortunately, there he was and here he is today, in all of our arguments, in our politics, in our religions, in our military attitudes, and in our moral judgments.

These are facts which I think we should all be aware of and keep in view as we make our decisions and policies in the future.

MEET THE AUTHOR

Richard Edward Noble was raised in Lawrence, Massachusetts. He attended St. Rita's grammar school in Lawrence, Central Catholic high school also in Lawrence, Northern Essex Community College in Haverhill and Merrimack College in North Andover.

His mother and father and grandparents – on both sides of the family – were Lawrence textile workers.

Richard lived in Lawrence until the age of twenty-seven and then migrated to Fort Lauderdale, Florida where he met his wife Carol. Richard and Carol have been a team for over forty years.

Richard has been a truck driver, a butcher, a boner, a breakdown man, a dishwasher, an oysterman, a fruit picker, a restaurant manager, a chef, a small butcher shop owner, a Kirby vacuum cleaner salesman, a fry cook, a broiler man, an expediter, a restaurant line boss, a hole digger, a swill collector for a pig farm, a raw bar man, a sous-chef, a tomato sorter, a sander in a spray paint factory and the owner/operator of an ice cream parlor and sandwich shop in Carrabelle, Florida. These experiences and many more were published in *Hobo-ing America – A workingman's tour of the U.S.A.*

Richard is now retired and working as a writer. He writes fiction, non-fiction and poetry. He published a column in a local newspaper. In 2007 he received a first place award for humor from the Florida Press Association for this column.

Richard has a variety of interests – philosophy, history, politics, the American and world labor movements, economics, poetry, music, biography, autobiography and the unique history of Lawrence, Massachusetts.

CPSIA information can be obtained at www.ICGtesting.com
Printed in the USA
BVOW04s1739290615

406662BV00001B/110/P